THE WORLD'S GREAT SERMONS

GUTHRIE TO MOSLEY

Volume V

Compiled by

GRENVILLE KLEISER

With an Introduction by

LEWIS O. BRASTOW

First published in 1908

British Library Cataloguing-in-Publication Data
A catalogue record for this book is available
from the British Library

CONTENTS

"The Lord Jesus Christ is the great Friend to whom we must all look for help, both for time and eternity."

—JOHN CHARLES RYLE

PREFACE

The aim in preparing this work has been to bring together the best examples of the products of the pulpit through the Christian centuries, and to present these masterpieces in attractive and convenient form. It is believed that they will be found valuable as instruction to ministers of to-day. They should also be helpful to others who, tho not preachers, yet seek reading of this kind for the upbuilding of personal character and for strengthening their Christian faith.

The sermons have been chosen in some cases for their literary and rhetorical excellences, but in every case for their helpfulness in solving some of the problems of Christian living. No two persons are likely to agree upon "the best" of anything, and readers will probably wish in particular instances that some other clergymen or sermons had been included. It is confidently believed, however, that the list here given is fairly representative of the preaching that characterized the age to which each sermon respectively belongs.

While some of the sermons of the early centuries may not seem exactly fitted to modern needs, it is thought that those presented will repay careful perusal, since they each contain a distinct message for later generations. Moreover, a comparison extending over the whole field of sermonic literature, such as the preacher may make with this collection before him, should prove most valuable as showing what progress and changes have come over homiletic matter and methods. Such a comparison should in fact throw much light on the spirit and conditions of various homiletic periods.

In choosing sermons by living preachers considerable difficulty has been found, not only in deciding upon sermons, but upon preachers. The list might have been extended indefinitely. Whenever possible the preacher, when living, has himself been consulted as to what he considered his most representative sermon.

Thanks are due, and are hereby acknowledged, to numerous clergymen, publishers, librarians, and others who have generously assisted the compiler in this undertaking. Most grateful acknowledgment is also made to the Rev. Epiphanius Wilson and the Rev. W.C. Stiles for valuable editorial assistance.

GRENVILLE KLEISER.
New York City, October, 1908.

INTRODUCTION

Collections of sermons by noted preachers of different periods are not an altogether uncommon contribution to literature. Italy, Germany, Holland, France, Great Britain and the United States have in this way furnished copious illustrations of the gifts of their illustrious preachers. Such treasures are found in the Latin and even in the Greek Church. Protestant communions especially, in line with the supreme significance which they attach to the work of the pulpit, have thus sought to magnify the calling and to perpetuate the memory and the influence of their distinguished sons. Still more comprehensive attempts have been made to collate the products of representative preachers in different Protestant communions, and thus to bring into prominence various types of sermonic literature. It is in this way that the Christian world has come to know its pulpit princes and to value their achievements.

The collection contained in the volumes before us is, however, more varied and comprehensive, reaching as it does from the fourth to the twentieth century, than any collection known to the writer. In the selection Professor Kleiser has brought to his task a personal knowledge of homiletic literature that is the product of much observation and study during many years, and an enthusiasm for his work that has been fostered by close intercourse in professional service with preachers and theological students. He has had the assistance also of men whose acquaintance with homiletic literature is very extensive, whose critical judgments are sound and reliable and who may be regarded as experts in this branch of knowledge. These volumes, therefore, may be accepted as a judiciously selected collection of sermons by many of the most notable preachers of the ancient

9

and modern Christian world. Their value as illustrating varieties of gift, diversities of method, racial, national and ecclesiastical peculiarities, and above all progress in the science and art of preaching, may well be recognized even by a generation that is likely to regard anything that is more than twenty-four hours old as obsolete.

LEWIS O. BRASTOW.
Yale University, New Haven, Conn.,
October, 1908.

GUTHRIE

THE NEW HEART

BIOGRAPHICAL NOTE

Thomas Guthrie, preacher, philanthropist, and social reformer, was born at Brechin, Forfarshire, Scotland, in 1803. He spent ten years at the University of Edinburgh and was licensed to preach by the Presbytery of Brechin in 1825. In 1830 he was ordained minister of Arbirlot. After a valuable experience in evangelical preaching among the farmers, weavers and peasants of his congregation, he became one of the ministers of Old Greyfriars Church, Edinburgh, in 1827. Lord Cockburn described his sermons in that city as appealing equally "to the poor woman on the steps of the pulpit" as to the "stranger attracted solely by his eloquence." He was a great temperance advocate, becoming a total abstainer in 1844, and has been styled "the apostle of the ragged school movement." Retiring from the active work of the ministry in 1864, he still remained in public life until he died in 1873. Through long practise, Dr. Guthrie delivered his memorized discourses as tho they fell spontaneously from his lips. His voice has been described as powerful and musical. He was fond of vivid illustration, and even on his death bed, as he lay dying in the arms of his sons, he exclaimed: "I am just as helpless in your arms now as you once were in mine."

GUTHRIE

1803-1873

THE NEW HEART

A new heart also will I give you, and a new spirit will I put within you; and I will take away the stony heart out of your flesh, and I will give you an heart of flesh.—Ezekiel xxxvi., 26.

As in a machine where the parts all fit each other, and, bathed in oil, move without din or discord, the most perfect harmony reigns throughout the kingdom of grace. Jesus Christ is the "wisdom," as well as the "power" of God; nor in this kingdom is anything found corresponding to the anomalies and incongruities of the world lying without. There we sometimes see a high station disgraced by a man of low habits; while others are doomed to an inferior condition, who would shine like gilded ornaments on the very pinnacles of society. That beautiful congruity in Christ's kingdom is secured by those who are the objects of saving mercy being so renewed and sanctified that their nature is in harmony with their position, and the man within corresponds to all without.

Observe how this property of "new" runs through the whole economy of grace. When mercy first rose upon this world, an attribute of Divinity appeared which was new to the eyes of men and angels. Again, the Savior was born of a virgin; and He who came forth from a womb where no child had been previously conceived, was sepulchered in a tomb where no man had been previously interred. The infant had a new birthplace, the crucified had a new burial-place. Again, Jesus is the mediator of a new covenant, the author of a new testament, the founder of a new faith. Again, the redeemed receive a new name; they sing a new song; their home is not to be in the old, but in the new, Jerusalem, where they shall dwell on a new earth, and walk in glory beneath a new heaven. Now it were surely strange, when all things else are new, if they themselves were not to partake of this general renovation. Nor strange only, for such a change is indispensable. A new name without a new nature were an imposture. It were not more an untruth to call a lion a lamb, or the rapacious vulture by the name of the gentle dove, than to give the title of sons of God to the venomous seed of the serpent.

Then, again, unless man received a new nature, how could he sing the new song? The raven, perched on the rock, where she whets her bloody beak, and impatiently watches the dying struggles of some unhappy lamb can not tune her croaking voice to the rich, mellow music of a thrush; and, since it is out of the abundance of the heart that the mouth speaketh, how could a sinner take up the strain and sing the song of saints? Besides, unless a man were a new creature, he were out of place in the new creation. In circumstances neither adapted to his nature, nor fitted to minister to his happiness, a sinner in heaven would find himself as much out of his element as a finny inhabitant of the deep, or a sightless burrower in the soil, beside an eagle, soaring in the sky, or surveying her wide domain from the mountain crag.

In the works of God we see nothing more beautiful than the divine skill with which He suits His creatures to their condition. He gives wings to birds, fins to fishes, sails to the thistle-seed, a lamp to light the glowworm, great roots to moor the cedar, and to the aspiring ivy her thousand hands to climb the wall. Nor is the wisdom so conspicuous in nature, less remarkable and adorable in the kingdom of grace. He forms a holy people for a holy heaven—fits heaven for them, and them for heaven. And calling up His Son to prepare the mansions for their tenants, and sending down His Spirit to prepare the tenants for their mansions, He thus establishes a perfect harmony between the new creature and the new creation.

You can not have two hearts beating in the same bosom, else you would be, not a man, but a monster. Therefore, the very first thing to be done, in order to make things new, is just to take that which is old out of the way. And the taking away of the old heart is, after all, but a preparatory process. It is a means, but not the end. For, strange as it may at first sound, he is not religious who is without sin. A dead man is without sin; and he is sinless, who lies buried in dreamless slumber, so long as his eyes are sealed. Now, God requires more than a negative religion. Piety, like fire, light, electricity, magnetism, is an active, not a passive element; it has a positive, not merely a negative existence. For how is pure and undefiled religion defined? "Pure religion and undefiled is to visit the fatherless and widows in their affliction." And on whom does Jesus pronounce His beatitude? "If ye know these things, happy are ye if ye do them." And what is the sum of practical piety—the most portable form in which you can put an answer to Saul's question, "Lord, what wouldst thou have me to do?" What but this, "Depart from evil, and do good." Therefore, while God promises to take the stony heart out of our flesh, He promises more. In taking away one heart, He engages to supply us with another; and to this further change and onward stage in the process of redemption, I now proceed to turn your attention.

By way of general observation, I remark that our affections are engaged in religion. An oak—not as it stands choked up in the crowded wood, with room neither to spread nor breathe, but as it stands in the open field, swelling out below where it anchors its roots in the ground, and swelling out above where it stretches its arms into the air,—presents us with the most perfect form of firmness, self-support, stout and sturdy independence. So perfectly formed, indeed, is the monarch of the forest to stand alone, and fight its own battles with the elements, that the architect of the Bell Rock lighthouse is said to have borrowed his idea of its form from God in nature, and that, copying the work of a divine Architect, he took the trunk of the oak as the model of a building which was to stand the blast of the storm, and the swell of the winter seas.

Observe, that although the state of the natural affections does not furnish any certain evidence of conversion, it is the glory of piety that these are strengthened, elevated, sanctified by the change. The lover of God will be the kindest, best, wisest lover of his fellow-creatures. The heart that has room in it for God, grows so large, that it finds room for all God's train, for all that He loves, and for all that He has made; so that the Church, with all its denominations of true Christians, the world, with all its perishing sinners, nay, all the worlds which He has created, find orbit-room to move, as in an expansive universe, within the capacious enlargement of a believer's heart. For while the love of sin acts as an astringent—contracting the dimensions of the natural heart, shutting and shriveling it up—the love of God expands and enlarges its capacity. Piety quickens the pulse of love, warms and strengthens our heart, and sends forth fuller streams of natural affection toward all that have a claim on us, just as a strong and healthy heart sends tides of blood along the elastic arteries to every extremity of the body.

This new heart, however, mainly consists in a change of the affections as they regard spiritual objects. Without again traveling over ground which we have already surveyed, just look at the heart and feelings of an unconverted man. His mind being carnal, is enmity or hatred against God. This may be latent, not at first sight apparent, nor suspected, but how soon does it appear when put to the proof? Fairly tried, it comes out like those unseen elements which chemical tests reveal. Let God, for instance, by His providences or laws, thwart the wishes or cross the propensities of our unrenewed nature—let there be a collision between His will and ours—and the latent enmity flashes out like latent fire when the cold black flint is struck with steel.

In conversion God gives a new spirit. Conversion does not bestow new faculties. It does not turn a weak man into a philosopher. Yet, along with our affections, the temper, the will, the judgment partake of this great and holy change. Thus, while the heart ceases to be dead, the head, illuminated by a light within, ceases to be dark; the understanding is enlightened; the will is renewed; and our whole temper is sweetened and sanctified by the Spirit of God. To consider these in their order, I remark—

By this change the understanding and judgment are enlightened. Sin is the greatest folly, and the sinner the greatest fool in the world. There is no such madness in the most fitful lunacy. Think of a man risking eternity and his everlasting happiness on the uncertain chance of surviving another year. Think of a man purchasing a momentary pleasure at the cost of endless pain. Think of a dying man living as if he were never to die. Is there a convert to God who looks back upon his unconverted state, and does not say with David, "Lord, I was as a beast before Thee."

Now conversion not only restores God to the heart, but reason also to her throne. Time and eternity are now seen in their just proportions—in their right relative dimensions; the one in its littleness, and the other in its greatness. When the light of heaven rises on the soul, what grand discoveries does she make—of the exceeding evil of sin, of the holiness of the divine law, of the infinite purity of divine justice, of the grace and greatness of divine love. On Sinai's summit and on Calvary's cross, what new, sublime, affecting scenes open on her astonished eyes! She now, as by one convulsive bound, leaps to the conclusion that salvation is the one thing needful, and that if a man will give all he hath for the life that now is, much more should he part with all for the life to come. The Savior and Satan, the soul and body, holiness and sin, have competing claims. Between these reason now holds the balance even, and man finds, in the visit of converting grace, what the demoniac found in Jesus' advent. The man whose dwelling was among the tombs, whom no chains could bind, is seated at the feet of Jesus, "clothed, and in his right mind."

By this change the will is renewed. Bad men are worse, and good men are better than they appear. In conversion the will is so changed and sanctified, that altho a pious man is in some respects less, in other respects he is more holy than the world gives him credit for. The attainments of a believer are always beneath his aims; his desires are nobler than his deeds; his wishes are holier than his works. Give other men their will, full swing to their passions, and they would be worse than they are; give that to him, and he would be better than he is. And if you have experienced the gracious change, it will be your daily grief that you are not what you not only know you should be, but what you wish to be. To be complaining with Paul, "When I would do good, evil is present with me; that which I would I do not, and what I would not, that I do," is one of the best evidences of a gracious, saving change.

Children of God! let not your souls be cast down. This struggle between the new will and the old man—painful and prolonged altho it be—proves beyond all doubt the advent of the Holy Spirit. Until the Savior appeared there was no sword drawn, nor blood shed in Bethlehem, nor murderous decree issued against its innocents—they slept safely in their mothers' bosoms, Herod enjoyed his security and pleasure, and Rachel rose not from her grave to weep for her children because they were not. Christ's coming rouses all the devil in the soul. The fruits of holy peace are reaped with swords on the fields of war; and this struggle within your breast proves that grace, even in its infancy a cradled Savior, is engaged in strangling the old Serpent. When the shadow of calamity falls on many homes, and the tidings of victory come with sad news to many a family, and the brave are lying thick in the deadly breach, men comfort us by saying, that there are things worse than war. That is emphatically true of this holy war. Rejoice that the peace of death is gone.

By conversion the temper and disposition are changed and sanctified. Christians are occasionally to be found with a tone of mind and a temper as little calculated to recommend their faith as to promote their happiness. I believe that there are cases in which this is due to a deranged condition of the nervous system, or the presence of disease in some other vital organ. These unhappy persons are more deserving of our pity than our censure. This is not only the judgment of Christian charity, but of sound philosophy, and is a conclusion to which we are conducted in studying the union between mind and body, and the manner in which they act and re-act upon each other. So long as grace dwells in a "vile body," which is the seat of frequent disorder and many diseases—these infirmities of temper admit no more, perhaps, of being entirely removed, than a defect of speech, or any physical deformity. The good temper for which some take credit may be the result of good health and a well-developed frame—a physical more than a moral virtue; and an ill temper, springing from bad health, or an imperfect organization, may be a physical rather than a moral defect—giving its victim a claim on our charity and forbearance. But, admitting this apology for the unhappy tone and temper of some pious men, the true Christian will bitterly bewail his defect, and, regretting his infirmity more than others do a deformity, he will carefully guard and earnestly pray against it. Considering it as a thorn in his flesh, a messenger of Satan sent to buffet him, it will often send him to his knees in prayer to God, that the grace which conquers nature may be made "sufficient for him."

I pray you to cultivate the temper that was in Jesus Christ. Is he like a follower of the Lamb who is raging like a roaring lion? Is he like a pardoned criminal who sits moping with a cloud upon his brow? Is he like an heir of heaven, like a man destined to a crown, who is vexed and fretted with some petty loss? Is he like one in whose bosom the dove of heaven is nestling, who is full of all manner of bile and bitterness? Oh, let the same mind be in you that was in Jesus. A kind, catholic, gentle, loving temper is one of the most winning features of religion; and by its silent and softening influence you will do more real service to Christianity than by the loudest professions, or the exhibition of a cold and skeleton orthodoxy. Let it appear in you, that it is with the believer under the influence of the Spirit as with fruit ripened beneath the genial influences of heaven's dews and sunbeams. At first hard, it grows soft; at first sour, it becomes sweet; at first green, it assumes in time a rich and mellow color; at first adhering tenaciously to the tree, when it becomes ripe, it is ready to drop at the slightest touch. So with the man who is ripening for heaven. His affections and tempergrow sweet, soft, mellow, loose from earth and earthly things. He comes away readily to the hand of death, and leaves the world without a wrench.

In conversion God gives a heart of flesh. "I will give you a heart of flesh."

Near by a stone, a mass of rock that had fallen from the overhanging crag, which had some wild flowers growing in its fissures, and on its top the foxglove, with its spike of beautiful but deadly flowers, we once came upon an adder as it lay in ribbon coil, basking on the sunny ground. At our approach the reptile stirred, uncoiled itself, and raising its venomous head, with eyes like burning coals, it shook its cloven tongue, and, hissing, gave signs of battle. Attacked, it retreated; and, making for that gray stone, wormed itself into a hole in its side. Its nest and home were there. And in looking on that shattered rock—fallen from its primeval elevation—with its flowery but fatal charms, the home and nest of the adder, where nothing grew but poisoned beauty, and nothing dwelt but a poisoned brood, it seemed to us an emblem of that heart which the text describes as a stone, which experience proves is a habitation of devils, and which the prophet pronounces to be desperately wicked. I have already explained why the heart is described as a stone. It is cold as a stone; hard as a stone; dead and insensible as a stone. Now, as by the term "flesh" we understand qualities the very opposite of these, I therefore remark that—

In conversion a man gets a warm heart.

Let us restrict ourselves to a single example. When faith receives the Savior, how does the heart warm to Jesus Christ! There is music in His name. "His name is an ointment poured forth." All the old indifference to His cause, His people, and the

20

interests of His kingdom, has passed away; and now these have the warmest place in a believer's bosom, and are the object of its strongest and tenderest affections. The only place, alas! that religion has in the hearts of many is a burial-place; but the believer can say with Paul, "Christ liveth in me." Nor is his heart like the cottage of Bethany, favored only with occasional visits. Jesus abides there in the double character of guest and master, its most loving and best loved inmate; and there is a difference as great between that heart as it is, and that heart as it was, as between the warm bosom where the Infant slept or smiled in Mary's arms and the dark, cold sepulcher where weeping followers laid and left the Crucified.

Is there such a heart in you? Do you appreciate Christ's matchless excellences? Having cast away every sin to embrace him, do you set him above your chiefest joy? Would you leave father, mother, wife, children, to follow Him, with bleeding feet, over life's roughest path? Rather than part with Him, would you part with a thousand worlds? Were He now on earth, would you leave a throne to stoop and tie His latchet? If I might so speak, would you be proud to carry His shoes? Then, indeed, you have got the new, warm heart of flesh. The new love of Christ, and the old love of the world, may still meet in opposing currents; but in the war and strife of these antagonistic principles, the celestial shall overpower the terrestrial, as, at the river's mouth, I have seen the ocean tide, when it came rolling in with a thousand billows at its back, fill all the channel, carry all before its conquering swell, dam up the fresh water of the land, and drive it back with resistless power.

In conversion a man gets a soft heart.

As "flesh," it is soft and sensitive. It is flesh, and can be wounded or healed. It is flesh, and feels alike the kiss of kindness and the rod of correction. It is flesh; and no longer a stone, hard, obdurate, impenetrable to the genial influences of heaven. A hard block of ice, it has yielded to the beams of the sun, and been melted into flowing water. How are you moved now, stirred now, quickened now, sanctified now, by truths once felt no more than dews falling out of starry heavens, in soft silence upon rugged rock. The heart of grace is endowed with a delicate sensibility, and vibrates to the slightest touch of a Savior's fingers. How does the truth of God affect it now! A stone no longer, it melts under the heavenly fire—a stone no longer, it bends beneath the hammer of the word; no longer like the rugged rock, on which rains and sunbeams were wasted, it receives the impression of God's power, and retains the footprints of His presence. Like the flowers that close their eyes at night, but waken at the voice of morning, like the earth that gapes in summer drought, the new heart opens to receive the bounties of grace and the gifts of heaven. Have you experienced such a change? In proof and evidence of its reality, is David's language yours—"I have stretched out my hands unto thee. My soul thirsteth after thee as a thirsty land"?

In conversion a man gets a living heart.

The perfection of this life is death—it is dead to be sin, but alive to righteousness, alive to Christ, alive to everything which touches His honor, and crown, and kingdom. With Christ living in his heart, the believer feels that now he is not himself, not his own; and, as another's, the grand object of his life is to live to Christ. He reckons him an object worth living for, had he a thousand lives to live; worth dying for, had he a thousand deaths to die. He says with Paul, "I am crucified with Christ, nevertheless I live." In the highest sense alive, he is dead, dead to things he was once alive to; and he wishes that he were more dead to them, thoroughly dead. He wishes that he could look on the seductions of the world, and sin's voluptuous charms, with the cold, unmoved stare of death, and that these had no more power to kindle a desire in him than in the icy bosom of a corpse. "Understandest thou what thou readest?"

It is a mark of grace that the believer, in his progress heavenward, grows more and more alive to the claims of Jesus. If you "know the love of Christ," His is the latest name you will desire to utter; His is the latest thought you will desire to form;

upon Him you will fix your last look on earth; upon Him your first in heaven. When memory is oblivious of all other objects— when all that attracted the natural eye is wrapt in the mists of death, when the tongue is cleaving to the roof of our mouth, and speech is gone, and sight is gone, and hearing gone, and the right hand, lying powerless by our side, has lost its cunning, Jesus! then may we remember Thee! If the shadows of death are to be thrown in deepest darkness on the valley, when we are passing along it to glory, may it be ours to die like that saint, beside whose bed wife and children once stood, weeping over the wreck of faded faculties, and a blank, departed memory. One had asked him, "Father, do you remember me?" and received no answer; and another, and another, but still no answer. And then, all making way for the venerable companion of a long and loving pilgrimage—the tender partner of many a past joy and sorrow, his wife draws near. She bends over him, and as her tears fall thick upon his face, she cries, "Do you not remember me?" A stare, but it is vacant. There is no soul in that filmy eye; and the seal of death lies upon these lips. The sun is down, and life's brief twilight is darkening fast into a starless night. At this moment, one calm enough to remember how the love of Christ's spouse is "strong as death," a love that "many waters can not quench," stooped to his ear, and said, "Do you remember Jesus Christ?" The word was no sooner uttered than it seemed to recall the spirit, hovering for a moment, ere it took wing to heaven. Touched as by an electric influence, the heart beat once more to the name of Jesus; the features, fixt in death, relax; the countenance, dark in death, flushes up like the last gleam of day; and, with a smile in which the soul passed away to glory, he replied, "Remember Jesus Christ! dear Jesus Christ! He is all my salvation, and all my desire."

By conversion man is ennobled.

While infidelity regards man as a mere animal, to be dissolved at death into ashes and air, and vice changes man into a brute or devil, Mammon enslaves him. She makes him a serf, and condemns him to be a gold-digger for life in the mines. She puts her collar on his neck, and locks it; and bending his head to the soil, and bathing his brow in sweat, she says, Toil, toil, toil; as if this creature, originally made in the image of God, this dethroned and exiled monarch, to save whom the Son of God descended from the skies, and bled on Calvary, were a living machine, constructed of sinew, bone, and muscle, and made for no higher end than to work to live, and live to work.

Contrast with these the benign aspect in which the gospel looks on man. Religion descends from heaven to break our chains. She alone raises me from degradation, and bids me lift my drooping head, and look up to heaven. Yes; it is that very gospel which by some is supposed to present such dark, degrading, gloomy views of man and his destiny, which lifts me from the dust to set me among princes—on a level with angels—in a sense above them. To say nothing of the divine nobility grace imparts to a soul which is stamped anew with the likeness and image of God, how sacred and venerable does even this body appear in the eye of piety! No longer a form of animated dust; no longer the subject of passions shared in common with the brutes; no longer the drudge and slave of Mammon, the once "vile body" rises into a temple of the Holy Ghost. Vile in one sense it may be; yet what, although it be covered with sores? What, although it be clothed in rags? What, although, in unseemly decrepitude, it want its fair proportions? That poor, sickly, shattered form is the casket of a precious jewel. This mean and crumbling tabernacle lodges a guest nobler than palaces may boast of; angels hover around its walls; the Spirit of God dwells within it. What an incentive to holiness, to purity of life and conduct, lies in the fact that the body of a saint is the temple of God, a truer, nobler temple than that which Solomon dedicated by his prayers, and Jesus consecrated His presence! In popish cathedrals, where the light streamed through painted window, and the organ pealed along lofty aisles, and candles gleamed on golden cups and silver crosses, and incense floated in fragrant clouds, we have seen the blinded worshiper uncover his head, drop reverently on his knees, and raise his awestruck eye on the imposing spectacle; we have seen him kiss the marble floor, and knew that sooner would he be smitten dead upon that floor than be guilty of defiling it. How does this devotee rebuke us! We wonder at his superstition; how may he wonder at our profanity! Can we look on the lowly veneration he expresses for an edifice which has been erected by some dead man's genius, which holds but some image of a deified virgin, or bones of a canonized saint, and which, proudly as it raises its cathedral towers, time shall one day cast to the ground, and bury in the dust; can we, I say, look on that, and, if sensible to rebuke, not feel reproved by the spectacle? In how much more respect, in how much holier veneration should we hold this body? The shrine of immortality, and a temple dedicated to the Son of God, it is consecrated by the presence of the Spirit—a living temple, over whose porch the eye of piety reads what the finger of inspiration has written: "If any man defile the temple of God, him shall God destroy; for the temple of God is holy, which temple ye are."

MAURICE

THE VALLEY OF DRY BONES

BIOGRAPHICAL NOTE

Frederick Denison Maurice, English divine and author, was born in 1805. He was the son of a Unitarian clergyman, and after studying in Cambridge began a literary career in London, where his friend Coleridge and others persuaded him to take orders in the Church of England. In 1836 he was appointed chaplain to Guy's Hospital. In 1840 he was elected professor of English literature and history and in 1846 of divinity at King's College, London, but lost both positions in 1853 because of his radical views. He was professor of moral philosophy at Cambridge from 1860 until his death in 1872.

MAURICE

1805-1872

THE VALLEY OF DRY BONES

The hand of the Lord was upon me, and carried me out in the spirit of the Lord, and set me down in the midst of the valley which was full of bones, and caused me to pass by them round about. And behold there were very many in the open valley, and lo, they were very dry. And he said unto me, "Son of man, can these bones live?" And I answered, "O Lord God, thou knowest."—Ezek. xxxvii., 1-3.

We are naturally curious to know whether two contemporary prophets ever conversed with each other. In Micah we found such evident indications of sympathy with the mind of Isaiah as warranted the supposition that he was his pupil. I can not trace any signs of a similar relation, or indeed of any personal relation, between Jeremiah and Ezekiel. Tho they were passing through the same crisis; tho they had both to witness the evils which were destroying their nation; both to share its miseries; tho the false prophets were the common enemies of both; yet their circumstances, their character, and their work were entirely distinct, in some points even contrasted. Their very differences, however, show us that they were both alike prophets and priests.

The Book of Lamentations exhibits the spirit of the individual man Jeremiah more transparently than his longer book, which is so mixed up with historical details, with anticipations of a ruin not yet accomplished, with hopes, however faint and soon dispelled, of a national repentance. Most of those whom the prophet had denounced were banished or dead. Men could talk no more about the temple of the Lord, could boast no more that the word of the Lord was with them; the vessel which the potter was shaping had been broken to pieces. The sadness of the prophet, which had been checked sometimes by indignation, sometimes by the consciousness of a word which must still be spoken, of a work which must be done, became complete and absorbing. Heretofore his intense sympathy with his country might seem to be qualified by his lively apprehension of its crimes; now both feelings were blended into one. When he looked upon the desolation of the city there sat upon his soul a weight of sorrow and evil, as if he were representing his whole people, as if there was no wrong which they had committed, no evil habits which they had contracted, which did not cling to him, for which he was not responsible. And this was no imaginary fictitious state of mind into which he had worked himself. God had made him inwardly conscious of the very corruptions which had destroyed the land. If he had made any fight against them; if they did not actually overpower him and enslave him, this was God's work and not his; the promise of the covenant made with his fathers, which was as good for every one as for himself, was fulfilled to him. And now he was realizing the full effect of this discipline. The third chapter of the Lamentations, beginning "I am the man that hath seen affliction by the rod of His wrath," contains the climax of his experience. In the memorable passages which follow, the history of a life is gathered up. "I said, My strength and my hope is perished from the Lord; remembering mine affliction and my misery, the wormwood and the gall. My soul hath them still in remembrance. This I recall to mind, therefore have I hope. It is of the Lord's mercies that we are not consumed. They are new every morning; great is thy faithlessness. The Lord is my portion, saith my soul; therefore will I hope in him. The Lord is good unto them that wait for him. It is good that a man should both hope and quietly wait for the salvation of the Lord. It is good for a man that he bear the yoke in his youth. He sitteth alone and keepeth silence, because he hath borne it upon him. He putteth his mouth in the dust if so be there may be hope. He giveth his cheek to him that smiteth him, he is filled full with reproach. The Lord will not cast off for ever; but tho he cause grief, yet will he have compassion according to the multitude of his mercies for he doth not afflict willingly nor grieve the children of men."

Anything more individual than these utterances it is impossible to conceive; and yet it is just by these that one understands the sacerdotal work to which Jeremiah was called. There was no longer any temple. The priests as well as the princes had been for the most part carried away by Nebuchadnezzar. But there was a man walking about in the deserted city to which the twelve tribes had come up,—in the midst of the ruins of the holy place into which the sons of Aaron had gone with the memorial of their names on their breastplates,—who really entered into the meaning of that function, who really bore the iniquities of the children of Israel before the Lord;—one to whom it was given to translate the ceremonies and services of the divine house into life and reality. He had been taught more perfectly, perhaps, than anyone who had served in the temple, what was implied in its worship and sacrifices. He felt the burden to which those sacrifices pointed, the burden of individual and national sins. Yet, with that burden resting upon him, he could enter into the presence of the Holy One of Israel. He was sure there was a deliverance for his people as well as for himself; that there could not be one for him if there was not also one for them. Thus when part of his work was over, when he had nothing more to say in the ears of kings or priests or people, this office,—which had been so closely connected with his prophetical office, and which, if it had depended upon outward conditions, must have been more entirely at an end than that,—still remained in all its original power. And the words of the prophet remained to explain to all generations the spiritual character and acts of the priest.

The office of the priest must have seemed to be more utterly extinct for Ezekiel than even for Jeremiah. He was forcibly removed from all the associations of the temple while it was yet standing. When he was called to be a prophet to the captives by the river Chebar, he might have supposed that the earlier designation which belonged to him as one of the Levitical family, had been extinguished in the later one. Yet we have seen how he was instructed, at the very commencement of his work as a prophet, that the glory of Him who filled the temple was surrounding him in Mesopotamia as it surrounded him when he went up to present the morning or the evening sacrifice in Jerusalem. Such a vision was given him of that glory as he had never beheld in the holy place. He found that the earth,—that common, profane, Babylonian earth upon which he dwelt,—was filled with it. All the powers of nature, the forms of animals, man as the highest of the animals, the motions and order of the outward world and of human society, were pointing towards it. And the central object, the highest object which he could behold, tho there was an ineffable brightness beyond, was a Man upon a throne, One who could command him, in whose name he was to go forth, whose words he was to speak.

This was no isolated revelation or dream. The very name which the prophet thenceforth bore, the name by which he was to know himself, depended upon it. "Son of man, stand upon thy feet and I will speak unto thee," were the first words which he heard after he fell upon his face. That great title is bestowed upon him through all the time in which he was prophesying. It was in many ways more suitable to him than to those who had gone before him. There was now no Hezekiah or Josiah to represent the Divine king. The witnesses for the kingdom seemed to be at an end. Nebuchadnezzar was the lord of the earth. At such a time the natural position of the Jewish seer became a human position. The Israelite's glory was to be a "Son of man."

Yet he was not absolved from any of the obligations of the older prophets; he was not to expect a more willing or attentive audience among captives than they had found at home; briars, thorns would be with him; he must dwell among scorpions. Lamentations and mourning and woe filled his roll as much as that which Baruch wrote out for Jeremiah. And he must eat this roll; it must become a part of his very soul; its words must come forth living and burning out of himself.

He must understand, besides, all the fearful responsibilities of the prophet. He was to speak whether the men about him would hear or whether they would forbear. There were times when his tongue would cleave to the roof of his mouth, when he should be dumb and should not be to them a reprover. But when God opened his lips, the blood of those to whom he was sent was upon him; it would be required at his hands if they died in their iniquity and he had not warned them. He must submit to do all symbolical acts, however strange and fantastical they might seem in themselves, which might bring the feeling of coming judgments home to a sense-bound people. He must act a mimic siege, he must eat defiled bread; he must cut off his hair and weigh it in balances, if so the people could be made to understand,—in spite of their false prophets who spoke of coming peace and enacted their signs, which of course involved no discomfort or humiliation to themselves,—that the city would really be destroyed and the sanctuary laid waste. He was to persuade his brother captives that they were a remnant in which the nation still lived, a stock out of which it should hereafter grow and flourish, even tho they were most rebellious, dreaming of good things which would never come, not waiting for that good which God had designed for them. There was to be the same end in all the punishments which were coming upon the land and in all its deliverances. God was saying in all "I am the Lord."

This sentence recurs again and again in the prophecies of Ezekiel. It is the thought of his mind, the one which gives all the sublimity and all the practical worth to his discourses,—that the knowledge of God is the supreme good of man, and that the desolation of his countrymen has come from their not liking to retain it. He is transported in spirit to the temple. There the same vision of the glory of God which he had seen by the river returns to him. The light of it shows him, portrayed upon the wall of the temple round about, the abominable beasts and creeping things, and the idols of the house of Israel; what the ancients of the house of Israel did in the dark, every one in the chambers of his imagery; how the women were weeping for Tammuz; how the men were worshiping the sun towards the east. Whether such abominations as these were actually to be seen in the temple, or whether the prophet's eye opened by the divine Spirit saw that they were possessing the hearts of those who seemed to others, perhaps to themselves, to be worshiping the God of their fathers, it is clear that the mind of Ezekiel was led back to the place in which he had ministered, that he might be taught how little the sacred building could preserve the truth which was enshrined in it.

What Ezekiel has seen in the temple enables him to answer the elders of Israel when they come to consult him in his own house. Just what was going on among those who worshiped in Jerusalem, was going on in the hearts of those who sought his oracles. They were setting up idols there. They wanted to know what God would do with them or against them; they did not want to know Him. And therefore Ezekiel announces to them a great and eternal moral law, one of the most varied application; "God will answer you according to your idols." The truth which is presented to you, will be colored, distorted, inverted by the eye which receives it. The covetousness which you are cherishing will make the best and divinest word you hear, a minister of covetousness. Your pride and your lust will make it a minister of lust and pride. No bolder or more awful paradox was ever enunciated than this, nor one which the conscience of everyone will more surely verify. And there was this special proof of courage in making such an announcement, that it must have destroyed Ezekiel's reputation as a prophet. The elders came in terror, feeling that they wanted guidance and expecting some ready-made answer, such as the regular traders in prophecy could always furnish. The truly inspired man answers, "I can tell you nothing,—nothing at least that will not deceive you and become a lie in your minds. For you bring lies in your minds, and except they be extirpated, they must convert whatever is added to them from without, to their own quality."

Ezekiel himself illustrates in another case this great principle. No commandment had established itself more completely by the experience of the people to whom it was addrest, than the second. The idolatries of the land had accumulated with each generation. Each had cause to complain of the last as bequeathing it a stock of corrupt habits and traditions; the sins of the fathers had been visited upon the children. These were facts not to be gainsaid. The captives had leisure to reflect upon them. It might have been a most profound and profitable reflection.

The use they made of it was to prove they were under a necessary law of degeneracy. How could they help themselves? The fathers had eaten sour grapes, and their teeth were set on edge. Who dared dispute it? There was God's own word for it. Had he not told them the plan and method of His own government? Such language addrest to one of the favorite preachers or prophets of the people, would have silenced him altogether. He would have said, "It is a mystery, no doubt; we must take the words of the commandment tho we can not understand them. God is Sovereign; He can do what He likes. If it pleases Him that each generation should be more corrupt than the last, we must submit and not dispute His will." Others there would be who would complain boldly and with good reason of a will that compelled to evil, but yet would lazily submit to it, supposing it to be inevitable, tho feeling the absurdity of calling it divine. Ezekiel boldly stands forth to dispute and deny the whole principle. He does not dispute or deny the second commandment,—that was probably the text of his discourse. But he will not let the second commandment or any other words in the world be pleaded against the character of God. Righteousness and equity he maintains to be the foundations of the divine character and of the divine acts. He will tolerate no resolution of them into a heathenish notion of sovereignty or self-will. "The ways of God are equal," he says, "and your ways are unequal." The sins of the father only descend upon the son, they are only punished in the son, when the son accepts them, entertains them, makes them his own. At any time he may turn round and repudiate them and cleave to the God who doth not will the death of the sinner, but desires that he should return and live. The doctrine of the second commandment and of the whole law, is that a man is righteous so long as he cleaves to the righteous God who has made a covenant with him, unrighteous when he forsakes that covenant and acts independently. Therefore the notion of any perpetuity in righteousness, or in evil, is equally cut off. Every man has the capacity of righteousness, the capacity of evil. Let him be ever so righteous, he must become evil the moment he ceases to trust in God and begins to trust in himself. Let him be ever so evil, he must become righteous the moment he begins to trust in God and ceases to trust in himself.

The enunciation of laws or principles seems more especially to belong to Ezekiel, as the experience of personal evil and the sympathy with national sorrow belong more to the tender and womanly nature of Jeremiah. Nevertheless, Ezekiel was to be a priest in this sense also, as well as in that higher sense of beholding the glory of God and proclaiming His name. Suffering was not the destination of one prophet; it was the badge of all the tribe. Ezekiel's life was to be a continual parable, illustrative of the life of the nation. A man scrupulously careful of the law, was to violate the precepts of it respecting food, and to eat what was loathsome. A man sensitive probably as to his reputation, and with that kind of lofty imagination which makes attention to details and all petty acts unspeakably painful, must submit, for the sake of his countrymen, to such as seemed most ignominious to himself and perplexing to them. Finally, the desire of his eyes must be taken from him with a stroke, and he must not mourn or weep. Even at such a time he must be a sign to the people, tho by doing so he should seem to refuse the sympathy that he most wants, and should only lead the captives to say, "Wilt thou not tell us what these things are to us that thou doest so?"

Apart from these sufferings which concern him individually and domestically, the vision of the desolation of Israel became every day more overwhelming to him. Nor was it only the desolation of Israel. He who was called "Son of man," was not likely to speak less of Egypt and Tyrus and the land in which he was himself dwelling, than those older prophets who had so many more reasons for regarding Judea as the one garden of the Lord. The arms of Nebuchadnezzar had been turning the earth upside down and making it waste. Everything must have seemed to him disjointed, incoherent, withered. Could it ever be renovated? Was it possible even for that country which God had blest above all others and man had curst above all others, to breathe and live again?

This was the question which was proposed to the prophet on that day when the hand of the Lord was upon him, and he was carried into the valley which was full of bones. The vision, clear as it is in itself, must not be read apart from the context of the prophecy. You should remember where Ezekiel was dwelling; by what kind of people he was surrounded; what was the condition of his own land; what had come and was coming upon all lands; or you will not understand the picture which now rose up before him. You should think, too, of the man himself, of the heat of his spirit, of the words which he had uttered in vain, of the acts which had only made the captives stare vacantly, of the desolation of his house and his heart. You should think of those other visions he had of the ascending scale of creatures, of the mysterious order of the universe, of the glory of God, before you place yourself beside him in the valley, and walk with him round about it, and look at the different bones, and see how each separately how altogether, they expound to him the condition of the house of Israel. It was dead,—that body from which he had believed that life was to go forth to quicken the universe. It had none of the beauty of a corpse in which there is still form, on which the spirit has left its impression. There had been a time of gradual decay, a time when the pulses of the nation beat feebly and faintly, but when they might still be felt; a time after that when you knew it had ceased to breathe, but when you could still speak of it as entire. But another stage had come, the stage of utter dissolution, when each limb looked as if it had nothing to do with any other, when you could scarcely force yourself to believe that they had ever been joined together. Can these bones live? what a thought to come into the mind of any man gazing on such a scene! It could not have come from himself, certainly, nor from any of these relics. God must have sent it to him; He must have led him to dream that such a resurrection was possible. And now the process of it is also revealed to him. The prophet is commanded to speak. His speech seems a mere sound in the air. But there is a noise and a shaking; then a frightful movement of the bones towards each other, each claiming its fellow to which it had once belonged. This strange effort at a union of dead things betokens a power that has not yet declared itself. And soon the sinews and the flesh come up upon them. They have acquired a form, tho they have no life. "Then said he unto me, 'Prophesy unto the wind; Thus saith the Lord God: come from the four winds, O breath, and breathe upon these slain that they may live.' So I prophesied as he commanded. And the breath came unto them, and they lived, and stood up upon their feet, an exceeding great army."

"Doth he not speak parables?" was the phrase by which the Jews of the captivity exprest their dislike and contempt for the troublesome and mystical prophet who was among them. "Doth he not speak parables?" is a question which men, looking round with weary hearts upon the condition of Christ's Church in various periods of its existence, have asked themselves, with a very different intention and spirit, when they have read this vision of the valley of dry bones. "Is not this written," they have said, "for the ages to come? Is not this one of parables concerning the kingdom of God?" Yes, brethren, if we will first read it fairly and honestly, as describing what Ezekiel says it described to him,—if we will not search for a distant application till we have acknowledged the immediate one,—we shall find that here, as everywhere, Ezekiel is exhibiting facts which belong to other times as well as his own, and laws and methods of a divine government which belong to all times as well as his own.

And that I may not waste your time in enumerating different crises of history in which the facts may be discerned, and by which the law and the method may be tested, I say at once, they are all for us; the vision and the interpretation are of this day. Do you not hear men on all sides of you crying, "The Church which we read of in books exists only in them. Christendom consists of Romanists, Greeks, Protestants, divided from each other, disputing about questions to which nineteen-twentieths of those who belong to their communions are indifferent. And meantime what is becoming of the countries in which these different confessions are established? What populations are growing up in them? Does the present generation believe that which its fathers believed? Will the next generation believe anything?" Brethren, you hear such words as these spoken. I do not mean to inquire how much there is of truth in them, how much of exaggeration, what evidences there are on the other side which have been overlooked; what signs of life there are anywhere in the midst of apparent death. But this I must say; Christians in general are far too eager to urge special exceptions when they hear these charges preferred; far too ready to make out a case for themselves while they admit their application to others; far too ready to think that the cause of God is interested in this suppression of facts. The prophets should have taught us a different lesson. They should have led us to feel that it was a solemn duty, not to conceal, but to bring forward all the evidence which proves, not that one country is better than another, or one portion of the Church better than another, but that there is a principle of decay, a tendency to apostasy in all, and that no comfort can come from merely balancing symptoms of good here against symptoms of evil there, no comfort from considering whether we are a little less contentious, a little less idolatrous than our neighbors. Alas, for this Church, or for any church, if its existence now, if its prospects for the future, are to be determined by such calculations as these! No, brethren, our hope has a deeper foundation. It is this; that when the bones have become most dry, when they are lying most scattered and separate from each other, there is still a word going forth, if not through the lips of any prophet on this earth, then through the lips of those who have left it,—yet not proceeding from them, but from Him who liveth for ever and ever, the voice which says, "These bones shall rise." It is this; that every shaking among the bones, everything which seems at first a sign of terror,—men leaving the churches in which they have been born, forsaking all the affections and sympathies and traditions of their childhood,—infidel questionings, doubts whether the world is left to itself or whether it is governed by an evil spirit,— are themselves not indeed signs of life, but at least movements in the midst of death which are better than the silence of the charnel-house, which foretell the approach of that which they can not produce. It is this; that all struggles after union, tho they may be of the most abortive kind, tho they may produce fresh sects and fresh divisions, tho they must do so as long as they rest on the notion that unity is something visible and material, yet indicate a deep and divine necessity which men could not be conscious of in their dreams if they were not beginning to awake. It is this; that there are other visions true for us, as they were for Ezekiel, besides the vision of dry bones. The name of a Father has not ceased to be a true name because baptized men do not own themselves as His children. The name of the Son has not ceased to be a true name, because men are setting up some earthly ruler in place of Him, or are thinking that they can realize a human fellowship without confessing a Man on the throne above the firmament. The name of the Spirit has not ceased to be a true name because we are thinking that we can form combinations and sects and churches without His quickening presence, because we deny that He is really in the midst of us. It is this; that when all earthly priests have been banished or have lost their faith, tho there should be none to mourn over the ruins of Jerusalem, or to feel its sin as his own, yet there is a High Priest, the great Sin-Bearer, ever presenting His perfect and accepted sacrifice within the veil, a High Priest not of a nation, but of humanity. It is this; that tho all earthly temples, in which God has been pleased to dwell, should become desecrated and abominable, tho all foul worship should go on in the midst of them, and tho what is portrayed on their walls should too faithfully represent what is passing in the more secret chambers of imagery, tho at last the shrines that have been supposed to contain the mystery which they set forth should be utterly destroyed, and a voice should be heard out of the midst of them, saying, "Let us depart,"—yet that this will not be the sign that the Church of God has perished, only the sign that the temple of God has been opened in Heaven, and that from thence must come forth the glory that is to fill the whole earth.

MARTINEAU

PARTING WORDS

BIOGRAPHICAL NOTE

James Martineau, an English Unitarian divine, was born at Norwich in 1805. He was educated for the Unitarian ministry at Manchester College, and in 1828 ordained to the Presbyterian ministry in Dublin. Resigning his pastorate in Ireland, he took charge of the Paradise Street Chapel in Liverpool, but on being elected to the chair of mental and moral philosophy in Manchester New College followed it to London 1853, succeeding J. J. Taylor as principal of the institution in 1868.

His sermons, delivered in the course of four years in the chapel of Manchester New College are specimens of combined eloquence and philosophical profundity, yet are, perhaps, most valuable for their ethical quality. He preached in Dublin, Liverpool, and London. He was a lofty and earnest soul, given to mysticism, a master of English style, and has been widely read. He died in 1900.

MARTINEAU

1805-1900
PARTING WORDS

Peace I leave with you: My peace I give unto you: not as the world giveth, give I unto you.—John xiv., 27.

This is a strange benediction to proceed from the Man of Sorrows, at the dreariest moment of His life; strange at least to those who look only to His outward career, His incessant contact with misery and sin, His absolute solitude of purpose, His lot stricken with sadness ever new from temptation to the cross; but not strange perhaps to those who heard the deep and quiet tones in which this oracle of promise went forth—the divinest music from the center of the darkest fate. He was on the bosom of the beloved disciple and in the midst of those who should have cheered Him in that hour with such comfort as fidelity can always offer; but who, failing in their duty to His griefs, found the sadness creep upon themselves; while He, seeking to give peace to them, found it Himself profusely in the gift. It was not till He had finished this interview and effort of affection, and from the warmth of that evening meal and the flush of its deep converse they had issued into the chill and silent midnight air, nor till the sanctity of moonlight (never to be seen by Him again) had invested Him, and coarse fatigue had sunk His disciples into sleep upon the grass, that having none to comfort, He found anguish fall upon Himself. Deprived of the embrace of John, He flew to the bosom of the Father; and after a momentary strife, recovered in trust the serenity He had found in toil; and while His followers lie stretched in earthly slumber, He reaches a divine repose; while they, yielding to nature, gain neither strength nor courage for the morrow, He, through the vigils of agony, rises to that godlike power, on which mockery and insult beat in vain, and which has made the cross, then the emblem of abjectness and guilt, the everlasting symbol of whatever is holy and sublime.

The peace of Christ, then, was the fruit of combined toil and trust; in the one case diffusing itself from the center of His active life, in the other from that of His passive emotions; enabling Him in the one case to do things tranquilly; in the other, to see things tranquilly. Two things only can make life go wrong and painfully with us; when we suffer or suspect misdirection and feebleness in the energies of love and duty within us, or in the providence of the world without us: bringing, in the one case, the lassitude of an unsatisfied and discordant nature; in the other, the melancholy of hopeless views. From these Christ delivers us by a summons to mingled toil and trust. And herein does His peace differ from that which "the world giveth"—that its prime essential is not ease, but strife; not self-indulgence, but self-sacrifice; not acquiescence in evil for the sake of quiet, but conflict with it for the sake of God; not, in short, a prudent accommodation of the mind to the world, but a resolute subjugation of the world to the best conceptions of the mind. Amply has the promise to leave behind Him such a peace been since fulfilled. It was fulfilled to the apostles who first received it; and has been realized again by a succession of faithful men to whom they have delivered it.

The word "peace" denotes the absence of jar and conflict; a condition free from the restlessness of fruitless desire, the forebodings of anxiety, the stings of enmity. It may be destroyed by discordance between the lot without and the mind within, where the human being is in an obviously false position—an evil rare and usually self-curative; or by a discordance wholly internal, among the desires and affections themselves. The first impulse of "the natural man" is to seek peace by mending his external condition; to quiet desire by increase of ease; to banish anxiety by increase of wealth; to guard against hostility by making himself too strong for it; to build up his life into a fortress of security and a palace of comfort, where he may softly lie, tho tempests beat and rain descends. The spirit of Christianity casts away at once this whole theory of peace; declares it the most chimerical of dreams; and proclaims it impossible even to make this kind of reconciliation between the soul and the life wherein it acts. As well might the athlete demand a victory without a foe. To the noblest faculties of soul rest is disease and torture. The understanding is commissioned to grapple with ignorance, the conscience to confront the powers of moral evil, the affections to labor for the wretched and opprest; nor shall any peace be found, till these, which reproach and fret us in our most elaborate ease, put forth an incessant and satisfying energy; till, instead of conciliating the world, we vanquish it; and rather than sit still, in the sickness of luxury, for it to amuse our perceptions, we precipitate ourselves upon it to mold it into a new creation. Attempt to make all smooth and pleasant without, and you thereby create the most corroding of anxieties, and stimulate the most insatiable of appetites within. But let there be harmony within, let no clamors of self drown the voice which is entitled to authority there; let us set forth on the mission of duty, resolved to live for it alone, to close with every resistance that obstructs it, and march through every peril that awaits it; and in the consciousness of immortal power, the sense of mortal ill will vanish; and the peace of God well nigh extinguish the sufferings of the man. "In the world we may have tribulation; in Christ we shall have peace."

This peace, so remote from torpor, arising, indeed, from the intense action of the greatest of all ideas, those of duty, of immortality, of God, fell, according to the promise, on the first disciples. Not in vain did Jesus tell them in their sorrows that the Comforter would come; nor falsely did He define the blessed visitant, as "the spirit of truth"—the soul reverentially faithful to its convictions, and expressing clearly in action its highest aspirings. Such peace had Stephen, when before the Sanhedrim that was striving to hush up the recent story of the cross, he proclaimed aloud the sequel of the ascension; and priests and elders arose and stopped their ears, and thrust him out to death; he had his peace; else how, if heaven of divinest tranquility had not opened to him and revealed to him the proximity of Christ to God, how as the stone struck his uncovered and uplifted head, could he have so calmly said, "Lord, lay not this sin to their charge"? Such peace had Paul—at least when he ceased to rebel against his noble nature, and became, instead of the emissary of persecution, the ambassador of God. Was there ever a life of less ease and security, yet of more buoyant and rejoicing spirit than his? What weight did he not cast aside, to run the race that was set before him? What tie of home or nation did he not break, that he might join in one of the whole family of God? For forty years the scoff of synagogues and the outcast of his people, he forgot the privations of the exile in the labors of the missionary; flying from charges of sedition he disseminated the principles of peace; persecuted from city to city, yet he created in each a center of pure worship and Christian civilization, and along the coasts of Asia, and colonies of Macedonia, and citadels of Greece, dropped link after link of the great chain of truth that shall yet embrace the world. Amid the joy of making converts, he had also the affliction of making martyrs; to witness the sufferings, perhaps to bear the reproaches, of survivors; with weeping heart to rebuke the fears, and sustain the faith of many a doubter; and in solitude and bonds to send forth the effusions of his earnest spirit to quicken the life, and renovate the gladness, of the confederate churches. Yet when did speculation at its ease ever speak with vigor so noble and cheerfulness so fresh as his glorious letters; which recount his perils by land and sea, his sorrows with friend and foe, and declare that "none of these things move" him; which show him projecting incessant work, yet ready for instant rest; conscious that already he has fought the good fight, and willing to finish his course and resign the field; but prepared, if needs be, to grasp again the sword of the Spirit, and go forth in quest of wider victories. Does any one suppose that it would have been more peaceful to look back on a life less exposed and adventurous, on a lot sheltered and secure, on soft-bedded comfort, and unbroken plenty, and conventional compliance? No! it is only beforehand that we mistake these things for peace; in the retrospect we know them better, and would exchange them all for one vanquished temptation in the desert, for one patient bearing of the cross! What—when all is over, and we lie upon the last bed—what is the worth to us of all our guilty compromises, of all the moments stolen from duty to be given to ease? If Paul had cowered before the tribunal of Nero, and trembled at his comrade's blood, and, instead of baring his neck to the imperial sword, had purchased by poor evasions another year of life—where would that year have been now—a lost drop in the deep waters of time—yet not lost, but rather mingled as a poison in the refreshing stream of good men's goodness by which Providence fertilizes the ages.

The peace of Christ, thus inherited by His disciples, and growing out a living spirit of duty and of love, contrasts not merely with guilty ease, but with that mere mechanical facility in blameless action which habit gives. There is something faithless and ignoble in the very reasonings sometimes employed to recommend virtuous habits. They are urged upon us, because they smooth the way of right; we are invited to them for the sake of ease. Adopted in such a temper, duty after all makes its bargain with indulgence, and is not yet pursued for its own sake and with the allegiance of a loving heart. Moreover, whoever has true conscience sees that there is a fallacy in this persuasion; for whenever habits become mechanical, they cease to satisfy the requirements of duty; the obligations of which enlarge definitely with our powers, demanding an undiminished tension of the will, and an ever-constant life of the affections. It can never be, that a soul which has a heaven open to its view, which is stationed here, not simply to accommodate itself to the arrangement of this world, but also to school itself for the spirit of another, is intended to rest in mere automatic regularities. When the mind is thrown into other scenes, and finds itself in the society of the world invisible, suddenly introduced to the heavenly wise and the sainted good—what peace can it expect from mere dry tendencies to acts no longer practicable and blameless things now left behind? No; it must have that pure love which is nowhere a stranger, in earth or heaven; that vital goodness of the affections, that adjusts itself at once to every scene where there is truth and holiness to venerate; that conscience, wakeful and devout, which enters with instant joy on any career of duty and progress opened to its aspirations. And even in "the life that now is," the mere mechanist of virtue, who copies precepts with mimetic accuracy, is too frequently at fault, to have even the poor peace which custom promises. He is at home only on his own beat. An emergency perplexes him, and too often tempts him disgracefully to fly. He wants the inventiveness by which a living heart of duty seizes the resources of good, and uses them to the last; and the courage by which love, like honor, starts to the post of noble danger, and maintains it till, by such fidelity, it becomes a place of danger no more. It is a vain attempt to comprize in rules and aphorisms all the various moral exigencies of life. Hardly does such legality suffice to define the small portion of right and wrong contemplated in human jurisprudence. But the true instincts of a pure mind, like the creative genius of art, frames rules most perfect in the act of obeying them, and throws the materials of life into the fairest attitudes and the justest proportions. He whose allegiance is paid to the mere perceptive system, shapes and carves his duty into the homeliest of wooden idols; he who has the spirit of Christ turns it into an image breathing and divine. Children of God in the noblest sense, we are not without something of His creative spirit in our hearts. The power is there to separate the light from the darkness within us, and set in the firmament of the soul luminaries to guide and gladden us, for seasons and for years; power to make the herbage green beneath our feet, and beckon happy creatures into existence around our path; power to mold the clay of our earthly nature into the likeness of God most high; and thus only have we power to look back in peace upon our work, and find a Sabbath rest upon the thought that, morning and evening, all is good.

But the peace which Christ left and bequeathed was the result of trust, no less than toil. However immersed in action, and engaged in enterprises of conscience, every life has its passive moments, when the operation is reversed, and power, instead of going from us, returns upon us; and the scenes of our existence present themselves to us as objects of speculation and emotion. Sometimes we are forced into quietude in pauses of exhaustion or of grief; stretched upon the bed of pain, to hear the great world murmuring and rolling by; or lifted into the watch-tower of solitude, to look over the vast plain of humanity, and from a height that covers it with silence observe its groups shifting and traversing like spirits in a city of the dead. At such times our peace must depend on the view under which our faith or our fears may exhibit this mighty "field of the world"; on the forces of evil, of fortuity, or of God, which we suppose to be secretly directing the changes on the scene, and calling up the brief apparition of generation after generation. And so great and terrible is the amount of evil, physical and moral, in the great community of men; so vast the numbers sunk in barbarism, compared with the few who more nobly represent our nature; so many and piercing (could we but hear them) the cries of unpitied wretchedness, that with every beat of the pendulum wander unnoticed into the air; so dense the crowds that are thrust together in the deepest recesses of want, and that crawl through the loathsome hives of sin; that only two men can look through the world without dismay; he, on the one hand, who suffering himself to be bewildered with momentary horror, and in the confusion of his emotions, to mistake what he sees for the moral chaos, turns his back in the despair of fatalism, crying, "Let us eat and drink, for to-morrow we die"; and he, on the other, who, with the discernment of a deeper wisdom, penetrates through the shell of evil to the kernel and the seed of good; who perceives in suffering and temptation the resistance which alone can render virtue manifest, and conscience great, and existence venerable; who recognizes, even in the gigantic growth of guilt, the grasp of infinite desires, and the perseverance of godlike capacities; who sees how soon, were God to take up His omnipotence, and snatch from His creature "man" the care of the world and the work of self-perfection, all that deforms might be swept away, and the meanest lifted through the interval that separates them from the noblest; and who therefore holds fast to the theory of hope and the kindred duty of effort; takes shelter beneath the universal Providence of God; and seeing time enough in His vast cycles for the growth and consummation of every blessing can be patient as well as trust; can resign the selfish vanity of doing all things himself, and making a finish before he dies; and cheerfully give up his life to build up the mighty temple of human improvement, tho no inscription mark it for glory, and it be as one of the hidden stones of the sanctuary, visible only to the eye of God. Such was the spirit and the faith which Jesus left, and in which His first disciples found their rest. Within the infinitude of the divine mercy trouble did but fold them closer; the perversity of man did but provide them to put forth a more conquering love; and tho none were ever more the sport of the selfish interests and prejudices of mankind, or came into contact with a more desolate portion of the great wastes of humanity, they constructed no melancholy theories; but having planted many a rose of Sharon, and made their little portion of the desert smile, departed in the faith that the green margin would spread as the seasons of God came round, till the mantle of heaven covered the earth, and it ended with Eden as it had begun.

Between these two sources of Christian peace, virtuous toil, and holy trust, there is an intimate connection. The desponding are generally the indolent and useless; not the tried and struggling, but speculators at a distance from the scene of things, and far from destitute of comforts themselves. Barren of the most blest of human sympathies, strangers to the light that best gladdens the heart of man, they are without the materials of a bright and hopeful faith. But he who consecrates himself sees at once how God may sanctify the world; he whose mind is rich in the memory of moral victories will not easily believe the world a scene of moral defeats; nor was it ever known that one who, like Paul, labored for the good of man, despaired of the benevolence of God.

Whoever then would have the peace of Christ, let him seek first the spirit of Christ. Let him not fret against the conditions which God assigns to his being, but reverently conform himself to them, and do and enjoy the good which they allow. Let him cast himself freely on the career to which the secret persuasion of duty points, without reservation of happiness or self; and in the exercise which its difficulties give to his understanding, its conflicts to his will, its humanities to his affections, he shall find that united action of his whole and best nature, that inward harmony, that moral order, which emancipates from the anxieties of self, and unconsciously yields the divinest repose. The shadows of darkest affliction cannot blot out the inner radiance of such a mind; the most tedious years move lightly and with briefest step across its history; for it is conscious of its immortality, and hastening to its heavens. And there shall its peace be consummated at length; its griefs transmuted into delicious retrospects; its affections fresh and ready for a new and nobler career; and its praise confessing that this final "peace of God" doth indeed surpass its understanding.

MANNING

THE TRIUMPH OF THE CHURCH

BIOGRAPHICAL NOTE

Henry Edward Manning, Roman Catholic prelate, was born 1808 at Totteridge in Hertfordshire and educated at Harrow and Oxford. After graduation in 1830, he studied for holy orders in the Church of England and was ordained in 1833. The Tractarian Movement was then at its height and Manning took a leading part in it. Appointed Archdeacon of Chichester in 1840 he took a commanding place as a preacher and leader. Newman's recession did not shake his allegiance, but the decision in the Gorham case, which gave the Crown the power of deciding doctrinal questions, drove him to seek refuge in the Roman Catholic fold in 1851.

He was ordained priest by Cardinal Wiseman and to the end of his life devoted himself to religious and philanthropic work in London. He was appointed to succeed Wiseman as Archbishop of Westminster in 1865. He was made cardinal in 1875. As a preacher he was logical and dogmatic, but his style is imaginative and his flights of eloquence tinged with poetic coloring and passion. He died in 1892.

MANNING

1808-1892
THE TRIUMPH OF THE CHURCH

We give thanks unto God, who maketh us always to triumph in Christ Jesus, and manifesteth the odor of the knowledge of Him by us in every place. For we are a good odor of Christ unto God, both in them that are saved and in them that perish; in the one indeed an odor of life, in the other an odor of death unto death.
—2 Cor. ii., 14-16. (Douay Version.)

Such was the confidence of the Apostle in the face of all that was most hostile, mighty, and triumphant in the judgment of this world. He was confident that through God his mission in the world was being accomplished, that the Word of God was triumphing over all the power of man. They may well have said to him, "What is this triumph you speak of? If this be triumph, what is defeat? You were stoned the other day in Lystra; you were imprisoned at Philippi; you were scourged at Jerusalem; you were saved out of the hands of the people only by Roman soldiers; you were confounded by the philosophers at Athens; and you were refuted out of the holy Scriptures by the Jews of Berea. If this is triumph, you are welcome to it." Such, no doubt, was the lordly and confident language of men in the face of the apostles of Jesus Christ then, and such is the language of confidence with which the world looks on the Catholic Church at this hour. It counts it to be a comedy played out, a stale medieval superstition, and a name that is trampled in the earth. In every age the Church has been militant and in warfare. It is under the same law of suffering which crucified its divine Head. His throne was a cross, and His crown was of thorns. Nevertheless He triumphed, and He triumphs still, and shall triumph to the end. And so at this moment, in this nineteenth century, in the century of modern civilization, of light, of progress, of scientific affectation, the Catholic Church is derided. They say to us, "Look at the Catholic Church in Germany; look at it in Italy; the head of the Church dethroned; and not a spot on earth for the incarnation to set its foot upon. If this be triumph you are welcome to it." Our answer is: "Yes, even now we triumph always and in every place. The Catholic Church is triumphing now in America, and in Ireland, and in the colonies of the British empire; aye, and in the midst of the confusions in Spain, and in France through revolution after revolution, and in the furnace of infidelity; aye, and in Germany, in the midst of all that the might of man can do against it; and in Italy too, where the head of the Church is morally a prisoner, it is triumphing even now."

But how can I verify this assertion? It would be enough indeed to quote the words of the apostle, but I hope to do more. The world esteems the triumph of the Church to be in wealth, power, glory, honor, public sway over empires and nations. There was a time indeed when the world laid these things at the feet of the apostles of Jesus Christ. There was a time when the Catholic Church and the Christian world knew how to sanctify the society of men; but there is this difference—the world then believed, and the world now is apostate. Nevertheless, there is a triumph in the Christian world and there is a triumph in the anti-Christian world; and what is it? It is that the Church in every age and in every condition, and in the midst of all antagonists, fulfils its mission and accomplishes its work, and no power of man can hinder it. Men may, as we shall see hereafter, to their own destruction, resist the mission of the Church, but its work will be accomplished nevertheless, and accomplished even in them; and its work will be a good odor of Christ unto God both in those that are saved and in those that perish. The world has neither tests nor measures by which to understand what the mission and the work of the Church are; but they who see by the light of faith have both. Let us examine, then, what is its mission, what is its work, and how it is fulfilled.

First of all, the mission of the Church among men is this—to be a witness for God, and for the incarnation of God in the face of the world. Our Divine Lord said of Himself: "For this was I born, and for this came I into the world, that I should give testimony unto the truth." As it was with Him, so it is with His Church; and therefore He said to His apostles: "You shall be witnesses unto me," and St. John said: "That which was from the beginning, which we have heard, which we have seen with our eyes, which we have looked upon, and our hands handled, of the word of life; for the life was manifested, and we have seen it, and do bear witness, and declare unto you, the life eternal which was with the Father, and hath appeared unto us; that is to say, the manifestation of God in the flesh, the incarnation of the Son of God." The Church was the witness of this divine fact to the world, and it is witness to this hour. I may say it is an eye-witness. It was eye-witness of what it declares. It was an ear-witness of what it affirms. I may say in truth that the Church of God, which testifies at this hour, saw the Son of God, and heard His words, and was witness of His miracles. So St. Peter expressly declares, speaking of His transfiguration: "We have not, by artificial fables, made known to you the power and presence of our Lord Jesus Christ; but we were eye-witnesses of his greatness. For he received from God the Father honor and glory, this voice coming down to him from the excellent glory: This is my beloved Son, in whom I am well pleased; hear ye him. And his voice we heard brought from heaven, when we were with him in the holy mount." More than this: it was a witness of the day of Pentecost, and upon it the Holy Ghost descended. It heard the sound of the mighty wind and it saw the tongues of fire. The Church therefore testifies at this day as an ear-witness and an eye-witness of the divine facts which it declares. And how can this be said? Because that which the apostles saw and heard they delivered to others who believed in them upon a full test and knowledge of their truth, and those who received their testimony held it as a sacred trust and declared it to those who came after. From age to age the testimony of the apostles has descended unbroken. The intrinsic certainty of their witness, resting on their own eye-witness and ear-witness of the facts, has not diminished by a shade, jot, or tittle in the lapse of time, and the external evidence of that fact has multiplied and extended throughout all time and throughout the world. Therefore the testimony of the apostles to these divine realities and truths is as living and fresh at this day as it was in the beginning. Then twelve men testified; now the nations of the world, united in one body by faith and by baptism, take up and perpetuate that testimony. And part of that testimony is this—that when the Son of God ascended into heaven, as they saw Him ascend, He fulfilled His promise that He would send the Spirit of Truth, the Holy Ghost, to abide with them forever; that when one divine Teacher had gone up to His Father's throne, another should come in His stead; that the world should never be without a divine Person and a divine Teacher in the midst of it; and that the Spirit of Truth by which they were united to their divine Head in heaven should unite them also to each other as His members in one mystical body, and should form to Himself a dwelling-place in which to abide forever. As the soul abides in the body of the man, so the Holy Ghost abides in the body of the Church. It is the sanctuary in which He dwells; the organ by which He speaks, so that the words of our Divine Lord are fulfilled to the very letter—"He that heareth you heareth me;" for the voice of the head and that of the body, as St. Augustine says, are one and the same voice. As they make one moral person, so their voice is identical, and the assistance of the Holy Spirit keeps the voice of the Church always in perfect harmony with the voice of its divine Head, fulfilling the promise of the Lord by His prophet: "My spirit which is upon thee and my word which I put in thy mouth, shall never depart out of thy mouth, nor out of the mouth of thy seed, nor out of the mouth of thy seed's seed from this time and forever." Thus, then, the mission of the Church is fulfilled always; whether the world believe or disbelieve, whether it gainsay or assent, it matters not; the testimony of the Church forever triumphs in every place.

Another part of the mission of the Church is this—to teach the doctrines of Jesus Christ in the midst of all the controversies and contradictions of men. In the face of all the errors and heresies of men there is one divine Teacher perpetually declaring the same immutable truth. In the clamor and confusion of the human voices of philosophers and human guides, of the scribes and Pharisees of the new laws, there is one divine voice—articulate, clear, and piercing—which cleaves through all the confusion, and is to be heard above the clamor of men and of nations—the voice of that one holy, Catholic, and Roman Church, spreading from the sunrise to the sunset, immutable in its doctrine, teaching the same truths identically in every place, and abiding always the same unchanging teacher in every age. This is a fact legible in human history. I need not offer proof of it from histories written by ourselves; it is proved by histories and controversies of those who are most opposed to us. There is an accusation which is repeated from age to age against the Catholic and Roman Church; and what is it? That it always persists in its old errors. I accept the accusation. Its persistence proves its immutability, and that which they account error we know to be the doctrine of Jesus Christ; because, as I have already shown from the Word of God, neither can the Catholic Church ever err in believing, nor can the Catholic Church err in teaching. These are two impossibilities, and they descend from one and the same divine truth. God, the Holy Ghost, abiding forever in the mystical body of Christ, illuminates the whole body of the faithful from the time of their baptism. From the time that the graces of faith, hope, and charity are infused into their souls, they are illuminated with the light of faith as the world is illuminated by the splendor of the sun at noonday; and the faithful throughout the world continue passively in their persistence in that one baptismal faith wherewith they were enlightened from their earliest consciousness. And further, they can never err in believing, because the Church which teaches them can never err in teaching. The episcopate throughout the world, which is the college of the apostles multiplied and expanded among all nations, has always the assistance of the Spirit of Truth to guide and preserve it, so that the errors of men and infirmities of our intellect never prevail over the light of faith by which the whole Episcopate and the Church is sustained in the revelation of the day of Pentecost. And more than this: nineteen general councils, from the first which declared the coequality and consubstantiality of the Son with the Father and the Holy Ghost, down to the last which declared the infallibility of the vicar of Jesus Christ,—those nineteen councils have been the organ of the Holy Ghost, preserving the truth in all ages; and the pontiffs, two hundred and fifty-seven in number, have also been guided and assisted by the same Spirit of Truth; so that no doctrine of faith and morals from their hand and from their lips has been out of harmony with the revelation of Jesus Christ. For these reasons the Church is fulfilling its mission, always and in every place, and it can say in every age, with a divine certainty of knowledge and with a divine authority of teaching: "It seemed good to the Holy Ghost and to us."

Once more, and lastly: there is another part of the mission of the Church which never fails, and is never baffled—and that is, that the Church judges between the truth of God and the errors of men, and gives decision with divine certainty what is truth, what is falsehood, what is light and what is darkness. Here again the world, in the confusion of its discordant witnesses, bears testimony to our truth. The world disclaims altogether the presence of any divine teacher in the midst of us. It derides the very notion. There is not a sect or a communion, or a so-called church, which lays claim to this divine guidance. They say infallibility exists nowhere but in God. As the Pharisees said: "Who can forgive sins but God only?" thereby acknowledging the divinity of Him who forgave the palsied man. And while they say: "We have no infallibility in us; we do not claim it; we deny its existence on the face of the earth," the one Teacher, who never varies in His voice, says: "He that heareth me heareth him that sent me." It seemed good to the Holy Ghost and unto us that we should claim that infallibility, and we cite you before the tribunal of God to answer for your denial of that truth. We say further that no man knows that any revelation was ever made to man except through our testimony. You never saw the Word made flesh, you nor your forefathers; and you have no unbroken succession of witnesses who trace upward these eighteen hundred years to the day when the Holy Ghost descended with wind and fire; you are not in contact with the original revelation of God. How can you rise up and say: "This was revealed upwards of eighteen hundred years ago," when you have no proof to give, except that which you borrow from me, that the Son of God ever came into the world? You take my witness for the fact of Christianity, and you then contradict me when I teach you what the doctrines of Christianity are. And if men appeal to the Scriptures, our answer is the same. How do you know the Scriptures were ever written? How can you prove that there ever was a book called the Word of God? You had it from me; you snatched it out of my hand, and you then read it and interpret it in contradiction to my teaching. How do you know that there were four greater prophets and twelve lesser in the Old Testament; that there were four evangelists and fourteen epistles of St. Paul in the New? Who told you all these things? You had them all from me—from me alone, to whom these Scriptures were committed in custody and in guardianship; from me, who preserved and handed them on to this day. You, who are denying the inspiration of this book and of that, of this text and of that text, and who are gnawing away, as a moth fretteth a garment, the whole written word of God, you rise up and tell us: "This is the meaning of the holy Scriptures," and you reject the holy Catholic faith.

Dear brethren, it needs great patience to hear these things;

nevertheless, the judge is always calm and patient while he is fulfilling his work among men, and that because it is a grave thing to be the odor of life unto life and of death unto death to the eternal souls of men. And when men appeal to antiquity and tell us that "this is not the primitive tradition," the Church answers: Were you ever in antiquity, or anyone that belongs to you? I was there, and as a perpetual witness antiquity is to me nothing but my early days. Antiquity exists in my consciousness to this hour, as men grown to riper years remember their childhood. Men of the world know that the contemporaneous interpretation of a law is the most authentic and certain interpretation. But I have the contemporaneous interpretation of holy Scripture; and more than this, men who practise before human tribunals know that the continuous usage of a country is the interpretation of its laws written and unwritten. But I have the contemporaneous and the continuous usage of the Church of God. The seven sacraments are institutions of Jesus Christ and every one of them interprets a cluster of truths. The existence of the Church itself is an interpretation of the words: "Thou art Peter, and upon this rock will I build my church, and the gates of hell shall not prevail against it." The jurisdiction that I have over the world, which the hearts of men recognize and to which their consciences respond, is the interpretation of the words: "Receive ye the Holy Ghost, whose soever sins ye forgive, they are forgiven unto them; and whose soever sins ye retain, they are retained."

But lastly there is another appeal which men make in this day. We are now told that scientific history is the test of truth; and I saw the other day in a document having great pretension from a certain body of men who are troubling Germany and attempting to trouble even England with the name of Old Catholics, that the way to know the pure faith of Jesus Christ is to interpret history by science. Alas, as I said before, the world is full of pretensions to science; but those who claim to be Catholics, and who yet appeal from the living voice of the Catholic Church to any other tribunal whatsoever, are all of them identical in their principle, and that principle is heresy. Luther appealed from the voice of the Catholic Church to Scripture, and thereby became a heretic. There are others who appeal to antiquity, and the appeal is the same—it is an appeal from the living voice, from the divine authority of the Church, to something of their own choice and creation. It matters not to what the appeal is made. That which constitutes both the treason of the act and the heresy of the principle is that they appeal from the living voice, that is from the divine voice. This it is that is being done at this moment by a body of men who profess to be and to intend to live and die Catholics; and what is more, to purify and reform the Church by staying in it. What is their appeal? Their appeal is to history, to scientific history; that is, to history interpreted by themselves. Luther was much more direct and much wiser. He appealed to a book which is certainly written by the Holy Ghost; they appeal to I know not what books, but to books certainly written only by men, and not by the Spirit of God; to human history, the authenticity of which and the purity of the text of which no one can guarantee; and even this they interpret for themselves.

Now bear with me further if I dwell a few moments longer upon this. At the time I speak, in the old Catholic city of Cologne there is assembled together a number of these men—some four or five hundred—with a handful of unhappy priests, perhaps six or eight, of whom the greater part had already the note of unsoundness upon them before they took their deadly step. And what are they? What are these men who are rising up to purify the Church? What do they believe? Some believe all the Council of Trent, but not the Council of the Vatican. Some believe the Church to be infallible, but not its Head; others propose to reject the invocation of saints, and purgatory, and compulsory confession, and I know not what. Others ask for either half or altogether rationalism. And who have they to assist them? Excommunicated Jansenists from Holland, and members, I grieve to say, of the Established Church from England; and those chosen, as it were, by a happy fatality, one the most extreme of old-fashioned high-church orthodoxy—an estimable and excellent man, whose person I both respect and love; and another whose advanced rationalism is such that even his own brethren can hardly forbear protesting against him. So that we have assembled in this congress, which is to reform and purify the Catholic and Roman Church of all ages, men so irreconcilably in contradiction with themselves that they cannot touch a religious doctrine without discord, and they cannot find anything on which to unite except in opposition to the one immutable truth. There was a day when all the Scribes, and all the Pharisees, and all the Herodians, and all the hypocrites, and all the men who could agree in anything else or at any other time, were united together in one conspiracy, and tho their witnesses did not agree together and their discordant voices could not be combined they all had one will and one purpose against the Son of God and against His truth. These men, I bear witness—many of them at least—have no such intention; but we know from the Word of God that neither had they who crucified our divine Master a knowledge of what they did: "Father, forgive them, for they know not what they do." "Which none of the princes of this world knew; for if they had known it they would never have crucified the Lord of glory." But they are at this moment fulfilling the very words of the apostles: "And to some the testimony of the Church is life unto life, to others death unto death."

Such then, is the mission and the work of the Church—to bear its witness, to teach and to judge; and in doing this, whether men will believe or whether men will not believe, it is accomplishing its triumph in the world. The world forgets that there is not only salvation, but there is also judgment; and God, the just judge of all, is putting men on their trial. The Church is fulfilling its office by proposing the way of salvation to men, visibly to the eye by its own presence, audibly to the ear by its own teachings, clearly to the intellect by the evident truth of its doctrines. It is putting men upon trial and applying the test to their hearts. It tests their faith to see whether men will believe; it tests their candor to see whether they will choose God above all things; it tests their courage to know whether they are ready to take up their cross and follow their divine Master. The Church says to the men of this day: "Whosoever will save his life shall lose it, and whosoever shall lose his life for my sake and the gospel shall save it." And in saying this God is separating between nation and nation and between man and man. His "fan is in his hand and he will thoroughly purge his floor and gather his wheat into the garner, but the chaff will be burnt with unquenchable fire." "He that believeth and is baptized will be saved; but he that believeth not is condemned." "We thank God, who always maketh us to triumph in Christ Jesus and manifesteth the odor of him by us in every place;" for we now, at this hour, in the midst of the nineteenth century, in the midst of science and progress, are the odor of life unto life and the odor of death unto death. For the purpose of God in the world is this—to gather out, as He did of old, a people for His name. Among the Gentiles of the old world He chose Israel; so now amongst the nations of the new world He chooses those that believe. He knows the number of His elect and He calls them by their name. He proposes to them the way of salvation and puts all things necessary—truth and grace— within their reach. God is putting them on trial, and the Church in this is fulfilling its mission and accomplishing its work.

The world is on its probation now. It has been for generations and generations driving God and Christianity out of its public life. Christianity is cancelled from its public law; Christianity is silent in the legislature; Christianity at this moment lingers in education, but men are endeavoring to close the doors of the schools against it and so to shut Christianity out of the knowledge of the rising generation. Wo to the people the tradition of whose Christian education is cut asunder! Wo to your children and to your posterity, if they are brought up without the knowledge of Christianity! The world is laboring with all its might, and all its fraud, and all its riches, and all its public authority, to accomplish this end. I do not say that the men who are doing it know what they do; but I affirm that they are doing what I say. Unbelievers like those who created the infidel revolution of France in the last century knew well what they were doing. "Let us destroy the accurst one," was the language in which they frankly spoke of Jesus Christ. Men are more refined in the present day. They talk only of the religious difficulty. "Let us evade or get around the religious difficulty;" and, under this plea of evading the religious difficulty, Christianity is to be excluded from our schools; that is to say, because grown men choose to controvert and contradict each other as to what is the truth of God, the little ones of Jesus Christ are to be robbed of their faith. Again, the world is separating its civil powers, its public authority from the unity of the faith and of the Church everywhere. It is making it a part of high and perfect legislation, of what we hear called in these days "progress and modern civilization," to separate the Church from the State, and the school from the Church. Progress has deposed the Head of the Church; it has put in derision a crown of thorns upon his head; and it believes that at last it has the whole world to itself.

This indeed is the triumph of the world. But meanwhile the Church is triumphing, tho men know it not. The Church was never more widespread than at this moment; never more luminous in the eyes of men, never more explicitly known in its faith; never more united, vigorous, pure, and confident in its work. Its kingdom is not of this world: that is, it is not derived from it; the foundation of its jurisdiction is in eternity; the source of its truth is in the Holy Ghost, and its imperishable Head is the Son of God at the right hand of the Father. His kingdom is in the world, but not of it. The world may prosper and go its way; it may stop its ears against the voice of the divine witness to the truth; nevertheless that witness will be the odor of death unto death.

And England also is on its probation. I bear witness that in England errors are vanishing away, as the snow melts before the sun—passing away, as the hard frosts before the coming of the spring. The errors which were once dominant, lordly, confident, and persecuting—where are they now? At this day men are proclaiming that they are not certain of what their forefathers bequeathed to them; that they cannot precisely tell what was the doctrine which was intended in the Thirty-nine Articles, and was incorporated in statute laws. They are no longer certain of these things; and I bear them witness that a gentler spirit and a kindlier disposition is working in the hearts of many. In the midst of this darkness, truth is rising again, and the old Catholic Church and faith, for which Ireland has stood inflexible as a martyr, with the aureola upon her head, at this day is multiplying the children of faith here and throughout the world. Here too in Lancashire, where the faith of England has never been extinct—where to this day the little children of our flock are the descendants of those who were martyrs and confessors some three hundred years ago—the lingering tradition of faith once more is embodied in the perfect hierarchy of the Church of God, in its perfect order, perfect unity, perfect jurisdiction, perfect authority. And, what is more, the men of England have learned to know it better. They have heard it speak; they have seen it worship; they have even knelt together with us before the same altar, perhaps hardly knowing what they did; and that because the Spirit of God is working for His truth, and multitudes will be saved. We are only in the twilight of the morning; but we can see Jesus standing on the shore, and there is a net in the hands of His apostles let down in the water. But when we are long gone to our rest, who can say what shall be the great draft of souls which shall be miraculously taken in England?

I must bear witness that in England there are tokens full of hope. England never rejected the holy Catholic faith. A tyrannous and guilty king, a corrupt and covetous court, men full of the conceit of false learning, schemers and intriguers, men that hungered to spoil the Church for their own enrichment—these tyrannized over the people of England. The people of England held to their faith and died for it. The people of England never rejected it. They were robbed of it; they were deprived of their inheritance, and their children were born disinherited of their faith; every century from that hour to this they have gone farther and farther from the light of the one truth. Poor English people! Bear with them—I speak as an Englishman—bear with them; they know not what they do in believing that we worship images, that we imbrued our hands in the massacre of St. Bartholomew. Let the men who write these things look at their own hands; there is blood enough upon them. But the English people do not believe these things now; they are passed away. And there has come in the place of these impostures a desire after truth—"Only let me find it;" a craving after unity—"Can we never make an end of these divisions?" a thirsting for the presence of Jesus Christ upon the altar—"Where can I find Him?" And what are all these aspirations? They are the evidences of the good odor of life unto life.

And if so, then, dear brethren, you that have the inheritance of faith are on your probation too. You are called to let the light of your faith shine like the day. The silent, penetrating, convincing light of a man who, knowing the faith, speaks it calmly, without controversy, without bickering, without contention, sheds a grace around him. As men that possess the greatest gift of God, and who desire to make everybody else share it to the full, so let your faith shine. And next, as you have faith, so you ought to have the warmth of charity. Where there is light, there is warmth; and where there is greater light there is greater warmth. Where there is perfect truth, there ought to be perfect charity. You who have the whole revelation of God ought to have the whole charity of God in you. Let your neighbors who are round about, even those who are not of the faith, feel that there is something in you—a warmth, a kindness, a sympathy and generosity which they find in no other man. And, lastly, let there be the fragrance of a holy life. This is the good odor of Christ unto God, and this diffuses life unto life wherever you go. You are upon this probation. Be worthy of the great gift which has been given to you. You have it in its fulness. Be then, worthy of its fulness, in faith and in charity.

And now, dear brethren, in the midst of all the lordly triumph of the world, of all that which no doubt we shall hear to-morrow, be of good heart. As they said to the apostles so they will say to us: "If this be triumph, what can be defeat? We do not quarrel if you are content with these victories." Overhead there is a throne, and round about it are those whom no man can number; the powers and prerogatives of Him who sits upon that throne are working mightily in the world. There is one who sits above the water-flood, with all its confusions, whose voice penetrates through all the jangling contradictions of men. He is bringing to its fulfilment the purpose which from all eternity He has predestined. He knows His own by number and by name, and He will gather them out as the shepherd gathers his flock, and He will separate the goats from the sheep. He will reign until the whole of that work is accomplished. When it is done, and when the last of His elect has been gathered in, and the last of His redeemed has been made perfect, then He will manifest Himself to all men, and the world shall then know that He has triumphed always and in every place.

PARK

THE PROMINENCE OF THE ATONEMENT

BIOGRAPHICAL NOTE

Edwards Amasa Park was born at Providence, R. I., in 1808. After a short pastorate of two years he became professor at Amherst, and subsequently at Andover Theological Seminary. He was one of the well-known exponents of the New England Calvinism, and his teachings had a wide influence over the ministers of his generation. His sermons, frequently rewritten, were marked by elegance of style and great moral force. Both as a preacher and teacher he showed largeness of view, depth of thought, and a rare facility of clear and powerful expression. He wrote a number of biographies and other works. He died in 1900.

PARK

1808-1900
THE PROMINENCE OF THE ATONEMENT[1]

For I determined not to know anything among you, save Jesus Christ, and him crucified.—1 Corinthians ii., 2.

Should the apostle who penned this eloquent expression resume his ministry on earth, and should he deign to hold converse with us on the principles of his high calling, and should he repeat his strong words, I am now, as of old, determined not to know anything among you save Jesus Christ, and Him crucified, some of us would feel an impulse to ask him:

"Can your words mean what they appear to imply? You are learned in Rabbinical literature; you have read the Grecian poets, and even quoted from Aratus; you have examined the statuary of Greece, and have made a permanent record of an inscription upon an altar in ancient Athens; you have reasoned on the principles of Aristotle from effect to cause, and have taken rank with the philosophers, as well as orators of the world; and now, you seem to utter your determination to abandon all knowledge save that which concerns the Jew who was crucified. You once said that you had rather speak five words with the understanding, than ten thousand words in an unknown tongue; and here, lest the pithy language of this text should fail of being truly apprehended, we desire to learn its precise meaning in three particulars:

"In the first place, do you intend to assert that our knowledge

---

1 Printed here by kind permission of Messrs. W. F. Draper & Co., Andover Publishing House, Andover, Mass.

is controlled by our will? You determined not to know anything save one. Can you by mere choice expel all but one of your old ideas, and make your mind like a chart of white paper in reference to the vast majority of your familiar objects of thought?"

"I am ready to concede," is the reply, "that much of our knowledge is involuntary; still a part of it is dependent on our will. In some degree, at some times, we may attend to a theme or not attend to it, as we choose, and thus our choice may influence our belief, and thus are we responsible, in a certain measure, for our knowledge. Besides, the word 'know' is used by us Hebraistic writers to include not only a mental apprehension, but also a moral feeling. When we know Christ, we feel a hearty complacence in Him. Again, to 'know' often signifies to manifest, as well as to possess, both knowledge and love. We do not know an old acquaintance when we of set purpose withhold all public recognition of him, and act outwardly as if we were inwardly ignorant of his being. But I, Paul, say to you, as I said to the Corinthians, that I shall make the atonement of Christ, and nothing but the atonement of Christ, the main theme of my regard, of my loving regard, and such loving regard as is openly avowed."

Thus our first query is answered; but there is a second inquiry which some of us would propose to the apostle, were he uttering to us personally the words which he wrote to the Corinthians. It is this:

"Should a Christian minister out of the pulpit, as well as in the pulpit, know nothing save the Crucified One? Did you not know how to sustain yourself by the manufacture of tents; and did you not say to the circle of elders at Ephesus, 'These hands have ministered to my necessities'? Did you not dispute with the Roman sergeants, plead your cause before the Roman courts? Must not every minister cease for a time to converse on the word of Jesus; and must he not think of providing for his own household, lest he become worse than an infidel?"

"I am willing to admit," is the reply, "that the pulpit is the place where the minister should speak of Christ with more uniform distinctness than in other places; but there are no places, and no times, in which he should fail to manifest, more or less obviously, his interest in his Redeemer. Wherever he goes he has a pulpit. Whether he eat, or drink, or whatever he do, he must do all for the glory of God, and the highest glory of God is Christ, and the highest honor of Christ is in Him crucified. A minister must always respect the proprieties of life; in honoring them he knows that appropriate model Man who, rising from the tomb, wrapped up the napkin that was about His head, and laid it in a place by itself. Now the proprieties of life do require a minister to speak in the pulpit on themes more plainly and more easily connected with the atonement, than are various themes on which he must speak in the market-place or in the schools. But all subjects on which he may discourse do lead, sooner or later, more or less obviously and easily, to the great work of Jesus; and he should converse on them with the intent of seizing every hint they give him, following out every line to which they point him, in the direction of the cross. I have been in many synagogues, and in the temple, and on Mars' Hill, and on a Mediterranean ship-deck; and once I was hurried along in a night ride from Jerusalem to Cæsarea with four hundred and seventy soldiers, horsemen and spearmen. I have resided at leisure with my arm chained to a Roman guard in a prison at the capital of the Roman Empire; but in all such places I have felt, and everywhere I do feel, bound to speak out, and to act out, all the interest which the fitness of the occasion admits, in the atonement of Jesus; and not to manifest, and not to feel, any interest in any theme which may lessen my regard for this, the chiefest among ten thousand!"

But there is a third question which some of us would propose to the apostle, were he to speak in our hearing the words of the text:

"Should every man, as well as every minister, cherish and exhibit no interest in anything but Christ? Should a sailor at the masthead, a surgeon in the extirpation of the clavicle, a warrior in the critical moment of the last charge, look at nothing, and hear of nothing, but the cross? Must not everyone conduct business, and sustain cares, which draw his mind away from the atonement?"

"I am ready to grant," is the reply, "that some duties are less plainly and less intimately connected than others with the work of Jesus; but all of them are connected with it in some degree, and this connection may be seen by all who choose to gain the fitting insight. The great principle of duty belonging to the minister in the pulpit, belongs to him everywhere; and the great principle of duty belonging to the minister, belongs to every man, woman, and child. There is not one religion for the man when he is in the temple, and another religion for the man when he is in the parlor or in the street. There is not one law for ordained pastor, and another law for the tradesman or the mechanic. The same law and no different one, the same religion and no different one, are the law and religion for the apostles, and publicans, and prophets, and tax gatherers, and patriarchs, and children, and nobles, and beggars. Every man is bidden to refuse everything, if it be the nearest friend, who interferes with the claims of the Messiah; and therefore every man, layman as well as clergyman, must keep his eye fixed primarily upon the cross. He may see other things within the range of that cross, but he must keep the cross directly at the angle of his vision, and allow nothing else, when placed side by side with the tree of Calvary, to allure his eye away from that central, engrossing object."

Here, then, is our third question answered; and in these three replies to these three queries, we perceive the meaning of our text to be: that not on the first day only, but on every day likewise, not in the religious assembly only, but in all assemblies, and in all solitudes likewise, not the preacher only, but the hearer likewise, every man must adopt the rule, to give his voluntary, his loving, his secret and open regard to nothing so much as to the character and work of his Redeemer.

Having inquired into the meaning of the apostle's words, let us proceed, in the next place, to inquire into the importance of making the atonement of Christ the only great object of our thought, speech and action.

And here, did we hold a personal interview with the author of our text, we should be prompted to put three additional queries before him. Our first inquiry would be:

"Is not your theme too contracted? It is well to know Christ, but in all the varying scenes of life is it well not to know anything else? Will not the pulpit become wearisome if, spring and autumn, summer and winter, it confine itself to a single topic? We have known men preach themselves out by incessant repetitions of the scene at Calvary,—a scene thrilling in itself, and on that very account not bearing to be presented in its details, every Sabbath day. How much less will the varying sensibilities of the soul endure the reiteration of this tragic tale every day and at every interview! Such extreme familiarity induces irreverence. The Bible is not confined to this theme. It is rich in ecclesiastical history, political history, ethical rules, metaphysical discussion, comprehensive theology. It contains one book of ten chapters which has not a single allusion to God, and several books which do not mention Christ; why then do you shut us up to a doctrine which will circumscribe the minds of good men, and result in making their conversation insipid?"

"Contracted!"—this is the reply—"and you consider this topic a limited one, whose height, depth, length, breadth, no finite mind can measure? Of what would you speak?"

"We would speak of the divine existence."

"But Christ is the 'I am.'"

"We would speak of the divine attributes."

"But Christ is the Alpha and Omega; He searcheth the reins and trieth the hearts of men; He is the same yesterday, to-day, and forever; full of grace and truth; to Him belong wisdom and power and glory and honor; of His dominion is no end. Of what, then, would you speak?"

"We would speak of the divine sovereignty."

"But Christ taught us to say: Even so, Father, for so it seemed good in Thy sight—and He and His Father are one."

"We would converse on the divine decrees."

"But all things are planned for His praise who was in Christ, and in whom Christ was at the beginning."

"We would discourse on electing love."

"But the saints are elect in Christ Jesus."

"We would utter many words on the creation of men and angels."

"Now by our Redeemer were all things created that are in heaven and that are in the earth, visible and invisible."

"We would converse on the preservation of what has been created."

"Now Christ upholdeth all things by the word of His power. What would you have, then, for your theme?"

"We would take the flowers of the field for our theme."

"But they are the delight, as well as the contrivance of the Redeemer."

"We would take for our theme the globes in space."

"But they are the work of His fingers."

"Then we would take the very winds of heaven for our theme, lawless and erratic as they are."

"But Jesus taught us to comment upon these as an illustration of His truth. His poetic mind gave us the conception that the wind bloweth where it chooseth to blow; and we look on, wondering whence it cometh, and whither it goeth, knowing only that it is the breath of the wonderful, the counselor, who arouseth it as He listeth, or saith, Peace, be still. What else, then, do you prefer for your topic of conversation?"

"We prefer the laws of nature for our topic."

"But in them the Father worketh and Christ worketh equally."

"If it be so, we will select the fine and useful arts for our subject."

"But all the materials of these arts and all the laws which compact them, and all the ingenuity which arranges them are of His architectonic plan. He is the guide of the sculptor, painter, musician, poet. He is the contriver of all the graces which we in our idolatry ascribe to the human discoverer, as if man had originally invented them. The history of the arts is the history of Christ's government on earth. Will you propose, then, some other theme for your remark?"

"Do let us converse on the moral law."

"You may; but Christ gave this law and came to magnify it."

"Then let us comment on the ceremonial law."

"You may; but all its types are prophecies of Jesus."

"Then we will expatiate on virtue in the general."

"Do so; but Christ is the first exemplar, the brightest representative of all abstract goodness, of all your virtue in the general."

"Then we will take up the ethical maxims."

"Take them up; but they are embodied in Him who is the way, the truth, the life."

"We will resort, then, to human responsibility for our subject of discourse."

"But we must all appear before the judgment seat of that fair-minded arbiter who is man as well as God."

"May we not speak of eternal blessedness?"

"Yes; but it is Christ who welcomes His chosen into life."

"Shall we not converse, then, on endless misery?"

"Yes; but it is Christ who will proclaim: Depart, ye cursed."

"The human body; we would utter some words on that."

"But your present body is the image of what your Lord wore once, and the body that you will have, if you die in the faith, is the image of what your Lord wears now; the image of the body slain for our offenses and raised again for our justification. And have you still a favorite theme which you have not suggested?"

"The pleasures of life are our favorite theme."

"Yes, and Jesus provided them and graced them at Cana."

"The duties of the household are our favorite theme."

"Yes, and Jesus has prescribed them and disciplines you by them, and will judge you for your manner of regarding them. What would you have, then, what can you think of for your choice topic of discourse?"

"We love to talk of our brethren in the faith."

"But they are the indices of Christ, and He is represented by them."

"We choose to converse on our Redeemer's indigent, imprisoned, diseased, agonized followers."

"And He is anhungered, athirst, penniless, afflicted in them, and whatsoever we do to one of them we do to Him, and what we say of one of them we say of Him."

"May we speak in the pulpit of slaves?"

"Of slaves! Can you not speak of Medes and Parthians, Indians and Arabians? Why not then of Africans? Have they, or have they not, immortal souls? Was Jesus, or was He not, crucified for them? Was He ashamed of the lowly and the down-trodden, and those who have become the reproach of men and the despised of the people? You may speak of all for whom Christ died; as all men, bond or free, and all things, globes or atoms, suggest thoughts leading in a right line or in a curved line to the cross of Christ. All things, being thus nearly or remotely suggestive of the atonement, are for your sakes; whether Paul or Apollos, or Cephas, or the world, or life, or death, or things present, or things to come,—all are yours, for your thoughts, for your words. If things pertain to the divine essence, the whole of that is the essence of Jesus; if they pertain to the divine relations, all of them are the relations of Jesus; if they pertain to the noblest and brightest features of seraphs, all the angels of God bow down before Jesus; if they pertain to the minutest changes of human life, in all our vicissitudes Jesus keeps up His brotherhood with us; if they pertain to the vilest and darkest spot of our depravity, they pertain to Jesus,—for to speak aright of sin is to be determined to speak of Christ and of Him crucified for sin.

"And is this the doctrine which men call a contracted one? Narrow! The very suspicion of its being narrow has now suggested the first reason why you should place it and keep it as the crown of all your words and deeds—it is so large, so rich, so boundless, that you need nothing which excludes it. And therefore," continues the apostle, "I mean to know and to love nothing, and to make it manifest that I care for nothing, in comparison with, and disconnected from, the God-man, as He develops all His attributes and all His relations on the cross."

But were the author of these laconic words in a familiar conference with us, we might be tempted to address to him a second inquiry:

"Is not your theme too large? At first we deemed it too small, but now it swells out before us into such colossal dimensions that we change our ground, and ask: Can the narrow mind of man take in this multiplicity of relations, comprehended in both the natures, and in the redemptive, as well as all the other works of Christ? Do not frail powers need one day as a day of rest, and one place as a sanctuary of repose, from every thought less tender than that of the atoning death itself? Must we not call in our minds from Christ and Him crucified, so as to concentrate all our emotions on the simple fact of Christ crucified?"

"Too large a theme!" this is the reply, "it is a large theme, too large to be fully comprehended by finite intelligences. Men have dreamed of exhausting the atonement by defining it to be a plan for removing the obstacles which stand in the way of our pardon. It is too large for that definition, as the atonement also persuades the Most High to forgive us. Then men have thought to mark it round about by saying that it is a scheme for inducing God to interpose in our aid. But the atonement is too large for that defining clause, as it also presents motives to man for accepting the interposition of God. Then some have thought to define it exactly, by saying that the atonement is both an appeal to the Lawgiver and also an appeal to the sinner. Too large still is the atonement for that explanation. It is an appeal to both God and man, but it is more. It is an appeal to the universe, and is as many-sided as the universe itself is to be variously affected. Can we by searching find out the whole of atoning love? It is the love of Him who stretched out His arms on the fatal wood, and pointed to the right hand and to the left hand, and raised His eyes upward, and cast them downward; and thus all things above and below, and on either side, He embraced in His comprehensive love. It is a large theme, but not too large to operate as a motive upon us. The immeasurable reach of a motive is the hiding of its power. The mind of man is itself expansive, and requires and will have something immense and infinite of truth or error, either overpowering it for good or overmastering it for evil. The atonement is a great theme, but not too great; and for the additional reason, its greatness lies, in part, in its reducing all other doctrines to a unity, its arranging them around itself in an order which makes them all easily understood. We know in other things the power of unity amid variety. We know how simple the geography of a land becomes by remembering that its rivers, altho meandering in unnumbered circuits around the hills and through the vales, yet pursue one main direction from one mountain to one sea. Now all the truths of God flow into the atonement. They are understood by means of it, because their tendencies are toward it; and it is understood by means of them, because it receives and comprehends them.

"Consider more fully the first part of this sentence; all other truths are understood by means of the atonement. It gives to them all a unity by illustrating them all. Other truths are not so much independent themes, as they are branches growing up or sidewise out of this one root, and they need this single theme in order that their relations may be rightly understood. What, for example, can we know in its most important bearings, unless we know the history and office of our Redeemer? Begin from whatever point we may examine the uses of things, we can never measure their full utility until we view them from the cross. The trees bud and blossom. Why? To bear fruit for the sustenance of the human body. But is this an ultimate object? The nourishment of the body favors the growth of the mind. But is the human mind an end worthy of all the contrivances in nature? Does the sun, with all its retinue of stars, pursue its daily course with no aim ulterior to man's welfare? Do we adopt a Ptolemaic theory in morals, that man is the center of the system, and other worlds revolve round him? All things were made of God, as the Being in whom they all terminate. Do they exist for elucidating His power? This is not his chief attribute. His knowledge? There is a nobler perfection than omniscience. His love? But there is one virtue imbedded as a gem in His love, and His love is but a shining casket for this pearl of infinite price. This pearl is grace. This is the central ornament of the character of Jehovah. But there is no grace in Jehovah save as it beams forth in Christ; not in Christ as a mere Divinity, nor in Christ as a mere spotless humanity, but in the two united, and in that God-man crucified. All things were made by Him and for Him, rising from the cross to the throne. Without reference to Him in His atoning love has nothing been made that was made in this world. The star in the East led wise men once to the manger where the Redeemer lay; and all the stars of heaven lead wise men now to Him who had risen above the stars, and whose glory illumines them all. He is termed the Sun of righteousness; and, as the material sun binds all the planets around it in an intelligible order, so does Christ shine over, and under, and into, and through all other objects, attract them all to Himself, marshal them all into one clear and grand array, showing them all to be His works, all suggestive of our duty, our sin, our need of atonement, our dependence on the one God, and the one Mediator between God and man.

"The first part of my sentence was, All other truths are understood by means of the atonement. Consider next the second part: The atonement is understood by means of other truths. It crystallizes them around itself, and reduces them into a system, not only because it explains them, but also because it makes them explain it. It is not too large a theme, for all the sciences and the arts bring their contributions to make it orderly and plain. Our text is a simple one, because its words are interpreted by a thousand facts shining upon it, and making themselves and it luminous in their radiations around and over it. Listen again to its suggestive words:

"'For I determined not to know anything among you save Jesus Christ, and him crucified.'

"Now, what is the meaning of this plain term 'Christ'? It means a 'King.' But how can we appreciate the King, unless we learn the nature of the beings over whom He rules? He reigns over the heavens; therefore we investigate the heavens. The whole earth is full of His glory; therefore we study the earth. He is the Lord over the angels; when we reflect on them, we catch a glimpse of Him in His regal state. He is the King of the Jews and the Gentiles. When we meditate on men, we enjoy a glance at Him who was born for this end, that He might have dominion over our race. When we contemplate the material worlds, all the vastness and the grandeur included in them—the sphere of mind, all the refinement and energy involved in it—we are overpowered by the reality, surpassing fable, that He who superintends all the movements of matter and first spake it into being and once framed, as He now governs, the souls of His creatures—He is the King who atoned for us; and the more we know of the stars in their courses, and of the spirit in its mysteries, so much the deeper is our awe in view of the condescending pity which moved their Creator to become one with a lowly creature acquainted with grief for you and me. So much is involved in the word 'Christ.'

"But our text speaks of Jesus Christ. That word 'Jesus!' What is the meaning of it? It means a 'deliverer,' and in the view of some interpreters it means 'God, the deliverer.' Deliverer? From what? We do not understand the power of His great office, unless we learn the nature and the vileness of sin; and we have no conception how mean, how detestable, sin is, unless we know the needlessness of it, the nobleness of the will which degrades itself into it, the excellence of the law which is dishonored by it. All our studies, then, in regard to the nature of the will, the unforced voluntariness of depravity, the extent of it through our race, the depth of it, the purity of the commands aiming to prevent it, the attractions of virtue, the strangeness of their not prevailing over the temptations of vice—they are not mere metaphysics; they are studies concerning the truth and the grace of Immanuel, who is God with us, and whose name is 'Deliverer' because He delivers His people from their sins; sins involving the power and the penalty of free wrong choice; a penalty including the everlasting punishment of the soul; a punishment suggesting the nature and the character of the divine law, and the divine Lawgiver, in their relation to the conscience and all the sensibilities of the mind; and that mind, as undying as its Maker. All these things are comprehended in the word 'Jesus.'

"But our text speaks of Jesus Christ and Him crucified: and this third term, 'crucified,' adds an emphasis to the two preceding terms, and stirs us up to examine our own capabilities—to learn the skill pervading our physical organism, so exquisitely qualified for pain as well as pleasure; the wisdom apparent in our mental structure, so keenly sensitive to all that can annoy as well as gratify; and thus we catch a glimpse of the truth, that He who combines all of our dignity with none of our guilt, and with all of the divine glory, and who thus develops all that is fit to be explained in man, and all that can be explained in God—He it is who chose to hang and linger with aching nerve and bleeding heart upon the cross for you and me. This cross makes out an atonement of the sciences and the arts and brings them also, as well as devout men, at one with God; all of them tributary to the doctrine that we are bought with a price—that we are redeemed, not with silver and gold, but with the precious blood of a man, who was God manifest in the flesh. Too large a theme is the atonement? But it breaks down the middle wall of partition that has kept apart the different studies of men; and it brings them together as illustrations of the truth, which in their light becomes as simple as it is great.

"The very objection, then, that the redemptive work is too extensive for our familiar converse, has suggested the second reason why it should be the main thing for us to think upon, and speak upon, and act upon: It systematizes all other themes, and gains from them a unity which becomes the plainer because it is set off by a luminous variety; and for this cause," continues the apostle, "I intend to know nothing with supreme love, except this centralizing doctrine which combines all other truths into a constellation of glories."

There is still a third inquiry which we might present to the author of our text, could we meet him in a personal colloquy:

"Your words all converge toward one point; will they not then become monotonous, and inapposite to the varying wants of various, or even the same, individuals?"

"A monotonous theme!" this is the reply: "What can be more diversified than the character and work of Him who is at one time designated as the omniscient God, and at another time as a Mechanic; at one time as a Judge, and at another time as an Intercessor; now a Lion, and then a Lamb; here a Vine, a Tree, there a Way, a Door; again a Stone, a Rock, still again a Star, a Sun; here without sin, and there He was made sin for us.

"Monotonous is this theme? Then it is sadly wronged, and the mind of man is sadly harmed; for this mind shoots out its tendrils to grasp all the branches of the tree of life, and the tree in its healthy growth has branches to which every sensibility of the human mind may cling. The judgment is addrest by the atonement, concerning the nature of law of distributive justice, the mode of expressing this justice either by punishing the guilty or by inflicting pain as a substitute for punishment, the influence of this substitution on the transgressor, on the surety, on the created universe, on God Himself. There is more of profound and even abstruse philosophy involved in the specific doctrine of the atonement, than in any other branch of knowledge; and there has been or will be more of discussion upon it, than upon all other branches of knowledge; for sacred science is the most fruitful of all sciences in logical deduction, and this specific part of the science is the richest of all its parts.

"Here, then, is the first method in which you may keep up the habit of making 'Jesus and Him crucified' the soul of your activity: Bring to your help the force of a resolute determination. There is a tendency in this resolute spirit to divert your thoughts from other themes, to turn the current of your sensibilities into the right channel, to invigorate your choice, to exert a direct and reflex influence in confirming the whole soul in Jesus. God is in that determination. He inspires it. He invigorates it. He works with it and by it. There is a power in it, but the power is not yours; it is the power of God. God is in every holy resolve of man."

In our interview with the apostle we should address to him a second inquiry:

"In what method can we avoid both the fact and the appearance of being slavishly coerced into the habit of conversing on Christ and on Christ alone? You speak of taking your stand, adhering to your decision; but this dry, stiff resolve-comes any genial spirit from it? Will you not be a slave to your unswerving purpose? Your inflexible rule, will it not be a hard one, wearisome to yourself, disagreeable to others? You hold up a weighty theme by a dead lift."

"I am determined"—this is the reply—"and it is not only a strong but it is a loving resolve. For the love of Christ constraineth me; whom having not seen in the flesh I love; in whom, though now I see him not, yet believing, I rejoice with the joy unspeakable and full of glory. It is not a business-like resolution. It is not a diplomatic purpose. It is not a mechanical force. It is an affectionate decision. It is a joyous rule. It is the effluence of a supreme attachment to the Redeemer.

"And this is the second method in which you may retain Jesus Christ as the jewel of your speech and life: Cherish a loving purpose to do so. A man has strength to accomplish what with a full soul he longs to accomplish. Your Christian toil will be irksome to you, if it be not your cordial preference; but if your undeviating resolve spring out of a hearty choice of your Savior, then will it be ever refreshed and enlivened by your outflowing, genial preference; then will your pious work be the repose of your soul. There is a power in your love to your work. It is a power to make your labor easy for yourself and attractive to others. This is not your power; it is the power of God. He enkindles the love within you. He enlivens it. He gives it warmth. He makes it instinct with energy. God is in all the holy joy of man."

In our conference with the author of our text we might suggest to him our third and last inquiry:

"In what method can we feel sure of persevering in this habitual exaltation of Christ? You speak of your stern purpose, but can you depend upon the continuance of it? You speak of your cordial as well as set resolve. But who are you? (forgive our pertinacious query). Jesus we know. But His disciples, His chief apostles—is not every one of them a reed shaken with the wind, tossed hither and thither, unstable as a wave upon the sea?"

"I know it is so"—this is the reply. "Often am I afraid lest, having preached the gospel to others, I should be a castaway. And after all I am persuaded that nothing—height depth, life, death, nothing—shall be able to separate me from the love of Christ; for I put my confidence in Him, and while my purpose is inflexible and affectionate, it is also inwrought with trust in the atonement and the intercession. I do pursue my Christian life in weakness and in fear and in much trembling. For all the piety of the best of men is in itself as grass, and the goodliness thereof as the flower of the field. Therefore serve I the Lord with all humility of mind and with many tears and temptations. Yet I am determined with a confiding love. I am troubled on every side; my flesh has no rest; without are fightings, within are fears; in presence I am base among you, my bodily presence is weak and my speech contemptible; and if I must needs glory, I will glory in the things which concern my infirmities. Still, after all, I am determined, my right hand being enfolded in the hand of my Redeemer. I know whom I have believed, and am persuaded that He is able to keep that which I have committed unto Him against that day. For my conversation is in heaven, from whence I am to look for the Savior, the Lord Jesus Christ, who shall change our vile body that it may be fashioned like unto His glorious body, according to the mighty working whereby He is able to subdue all things unto Himself. I say the truth in Christ; I lie not; I am the least of the apostles, that am not meet to be called an apostle, because I injured the Church of God; I am less than the least of all saints. Still I am determined; for by the grace of God I am what I am; and this grace which was bestowed upon me was not in vain, but I labored more abundantly than they all; yet not I but the grace of God which was with me; for I can do all things through Christ which strengtheneth me, and therefore I am determined.

"Borne onward, therefore, by your fixed plan, and no one can succeed in anything without a plan, yet you must never rely ultimately upon your determined spirit. Allured further and further onward by your delight in your plan, and no one can work as a master in anything without enthusiasm in his prescribed course, still you must not place your final dependence upon your affectionate spirit; for if you take, for your last prop, either the sternness or the cheerfulness of your own determination, then you will know your determination, and you are not to know anything save Jesus Christ and Him crucified. Here, then, is the third method in which you may give the fitting prominence to the best of themes: You must rest for your chief and final support on Him and only on Him, from whom all wise plans start, by whom they hold out, and to whom they all tend, who is all and in all, Jesus Christ and Him crucified."

My Christian brethren, you are all apostles. Every man, every woman, every child, the richest and the poorest, the most learned and the most ignorant of you—who have come up hither to dedicate yourselves and this sanctuary to your Lord, all being sent of Him to serve Him, have in fact and in essence the same responsibility resting on you as weighed on the author of our text. And he was burdened by the same kind of temptations and fears which oppress your spirit. But he was held up from failing in his work by a threefold cord; and that was his resolute determination, as loving as it was resolute, and as trustful as it was loving, to know nothing save Jesus Christ and Him crucified. The last that you hear of him as an impenitent man is in the words: "And Saul, yet breathing out threatening and slaughter against the disciples of the Lord." It was Christ whom the proud Jew last opposed. The first that you hear of him as a convicted man is in the words: "Who art thou, Lord?" It was Christ whom the inquiring Jew first studied. And the first that you hear of him as a penitent man is: "Lord, what wilt thou have me to do?" It was Christ to whom the humble disciple first surrendered his will. And the first that you hear of him as a Christian minister is: "And straightway he preached Christ in the synagogs that he is the Son of God." And the last that you hear of him as a Christian hero is: "I have fought the good fight, I have finished my course. I have kept the faith; henceforth there is laid up for me a crown of righteousness." And the secret of this victorious career is in words like those of our text: "I adhered to my plan (when among the fickle Corinthians), I was decided (when among the vacillating Galatians) to know nothing (when among the learned at Athens and them of Cæsar's household at Rome) save Jesus Christ (when I was among my own kinsmen who scorned Him), and Him crucified (when I was among the pupils of Gamaliel, all of whom despised my chosen theme); still I was determined to cling to that theme among the Greeks and the Barbarians, before Onesimus the slave and Philemon the proud master; for I loved my theme, and, suffering according to the will of God, I committed the keeping of my soul to Him in well-doing as unto a faithful Creator."

And herein is it to be your plan, my brethren, and your joy, not to make this sanctuary the resort of wealth and of fashion, but rather of humble suppliants, who by their prayers may divert all the wealth and fashion of the world into the service of your Lord; not to make this temple the resting-place of hearers who shall idly listen to the words of an orator, but a temple of earnest coworkers with Christ—thinking of Him, speaking of Him, loving Him first, and last, and midst, and without end. As you come to this house of God on the Sabbath, as you go from it, as your week-day recollections gather around it, may you renew and confirm your plan to know your Redeemer, and not only to shut yourselves up to the supreme love of nothing except Christ, but also—His grace will be sufficient for you—to worship and serve Christ in the central relation of Him crucified. Knowing Him alone, He will sustain you as fully as if He knew you alone. He will come to you in this temple as frequently as if He had no other servants to befriend. He will listen to your prayers as intently as if no supplications came up to Him from other altars, and He will intercede for you as entirely as if He interceded in behalf of no one else; for remember, that when He hung upon the cross, He thought of you, and died for you, just as fully as if He had been determined to think of no one, and to die for no one, save you, whom He now calls to the solemn service of consecrating your own souls, and your "holy and beautiful house" to the glory of Jesus Christ and Him crucified.

SIMPSON

THE RESURRECTION OF OUR LORD

BIOGRAPHICAL NOTE

Matthew Simpson, Methodist Episcopal Bishop, was born at Cadiz, Ohio, in 1810. He early distinguished himself as an orator, his style being that of spontaneous unpremeditated eloquence, in which he carried his congregation to heights of spiritual fervor and enthusiasm. He visited Europe in 1878 as delegate to the World's Evangelical Alliance in Berlin, which served to widen his reputation as a public speaker. He officiated at the funeral of Abraham Lincoln at Springfield, Illinois. His "Lectures on Preaching" delivered before the divinity students at Yale have been widely read. He died in 1884.

SIMPSON

1810-1884
THE RESURRECTION OF OUR LORD

But now is Christ risen from the dead, and become the first fruits of them that slept.—1 Cor. xv., 20.

A little more than eighteen hundred years ago, as the light of the morning was breaking around the walls of Jerusalem, there was a guard placed about a sepulcher in a small garden near the walls of the city. They were guarding a grave. Some strange scenes had occurred on the Friday before. While a man whom they had taken from the hills of Galilee and around the little lake of Capernaum had been hanging on the cross crucified as a malefactor, strange signs appeared in the heavens, and on the earth and in the temple.

It was rumored that he had said he would rise the third morning. The third morning was coming, and as the light began to break in the East, there came two women silently and sadly wending their way among the tents that were pitched all around the city of Jerusalem; they had sojourned all night in the tents, for as yet the gates of the city had not been opened. They came to see the sepulcher and were bringing spices in their hands. They loved the man who had been crucified as a malefactor, because of his goodness, his purity, and his compassion. They seemed to be almost the only hearts on earth that did love him deeply, save the small circle of friends who had gathered around him. There had been curses upon his head as he hung on the cross—curses from the by-standers, curses from the soldiers, curses from the people. They cried: "Away with him; his blood be on us and on our

97

children!" and on that morning there were none but a few feeble, obscure, heart-broken friends that dared to come near his grave.

A little more than eighteen hundred years have passed and on the anniversary of that day, the morning of the first day of the week, the first Sabbath after the full moon and the vernal equinox, at the same season, the whole world comes to visit that grave. The eyes of princes and of statesmen, the eyes of the poor and the humble in all parts of the earth are turned toward that sepulcher.

All through Europe men and women are thinking of that grave and of Him who lay in it. All over western lands, from ocean to ocean, on mountain top and in valley, over broad prairies and deep ravines, the eyes and hearts of the people are gathered round that grave. In the darkness of Africa, here and there, we see them stretching out their hands toward it. Along the coasts of India and the heights of the Himalayas they have heard of that grave and are bending toward it. The Chinese, laying aside their prejudices, have turned their eyes westward and are looking toward that sepulcher. Along the shores of the seas, over the mountain tops and in the valleys, the hearts of the people have not only been gathering around that grave, but they have caught a glimpse of the rising inmate who ascended in His glory toward heaven.

The song of jubilee has gone forth, and the old men are saying, "The Lord is risen from the dead." The young men and matrons catch up the glowing theme, and the little children around our festive boards, scarcely comprehending the source of their joy, with glad hearts are now joyful, because Jesus has risen from the dead. All over the earth tidings of joy have gone forth, and as the valleys have been ringing out their praises on this bright Sabbath morning how many hearts have been singing—

"Our Jesus is going up on high!"

Why this change? What hath produced such a wonderful difference in public feeling? The malefactor once curst, now honored; the obscure and despised, now sought for; the rising

Redeemer, not then regarded by men, now universally worshiped. What is the cause of this great change?—how brought about? The subject of this morning, taken from the associations of this day, call us to consider as briefly as we may the fact of the resurrection of Christ from the dead and some of the consequences which flow to us from that resurrection.

It is important for us to fix clearly in our minds the fact that this is one reason why such days are remembered in the annals of the Church as well as in the annals of nations; for our faith rests on facts, and the mind should clearly embrace the facts that we may feel that we are standing on firm ground. This fact of the resurrection of Christ is the foundation of the Christian system; for the apostle says: "And if Christ be not raised, your faith is vain, ye are yet in your sins; then they also which are fallen asleep in Christ will perish." If Christ be not risen, we shall never see the fathers and the mothers who have fallen asleep in Jesus; we shall never see the little ones who have gone up to be, as we believe, angels before the throne of God. If Christ be not raised, we are of all men the most miserable, because we are fancying future enjoyment, which never can be realized; but if Christ be raised, then shall we also rise, and them that sleep in Jesus will God bring with Him. And that our minds may rest as to the fact of Christ's resurrection, let us notice how God hath arranged the evidences to secure the knowledge of this fact clearly to man.

The first point to which our attention is invited is the fact of Christ's death. Were not this fact clearly established it would be in vain to try to prove His resurrection from the dead. Christ might have suffered for man in some obscure place; He might have laid down His life as a ransom, and yet there would have been no legal evidence of it. God allowed the wrath of man to become the instrument of praising Him, in that He suffered Christ to be taken under what was then the legal process—arrested first by the great council of the Jews, and then by the authority of the Roman governor, so that the matter became of public record—a legal transaction. The highest power, both of the Jewish and

Roman governments, united in this fact of His arrest, His trial, and His condemnation to death.

Not only was this permitted, but the time of the occurrence was wisely arranged. It was at the feast of the Jews, the Passover, when all the Jews came up to keep the Passover. They came not only from Egypt but from all the country through which they were scattered. Jerusalem could not hold the people that came together; they pitched their tents all around the city, on the hills and in the valleys. It was the time of full moon, when there was brightness all night, and they came together with safety and security. The multitude, then, was there to witness the scene, so that it might be attested by people from all parts of Judea and from all countries round about Judea.

Then, again, the form of the death was such as to be not a sudden one, but one of torture, passing through many hours. Had the execution been a very sudden one, as it might have been, the death would have been equally efficacious, yet it would not have been witnessed by so many; but as He hung those dreadful hours, from nine until three, the sun being darkened, what an opportunity was given to the people passing by to be imprest with the scene! The crucifixion was near the city; the crowd was there; the temple worship was in process; the strangers were there; and as one great stream passes on some festive day through the great thoroughfare of your city, so passed the stream of men, women, and children by that cross on which the Savior hung. They wagged their heads and reviled as they passed by. The very ones whom Jesus had healed, whose fathers had been cured of leprosy or fever, whose mothers' eyes had been opened; the ones who had been raised up from beds of sickness by the touch of that Savior, passed by and reviled, and said: "He saved others, Himself He cannot save." The multitude saw Him as He hung suffering on the cross.

Then, again, the circumstances attending His death were such as to invite universal attention. It was not designed that the death should be a private one; not merely a legal transaction, a matter soon over, but a protracted and agonizing spectacle—one to be seen and known by the multitude; but, in addition, that man's attention should be drawn to something to be connected with that wonderful scene; hence God called upon the heavens and the earth, the air and the graves, and the temple itself for testimony. It is said that before the coronation of a prince in olden time in Europe—and in some kingdoms the custom is still observed—there is sent forth a herald, sometimes three days in advance, at different periods according to the custom, to issue a challenge to anyone that dares to claim the kingdom to come and prove his right, and to announce that the coronation of this prince is to take place.

Methinks it was such a challenge God gave to all the powers of humanity and to all the powers of darkness. There hung suffering on the cross He who died for human wo, and as He hung God was about to crown Him King of Kings and Lord of Lords on the morning of the third day. He sends forth His voice of challenge, and as He speaks the earth rocks to its center; that ground, shaking and convulsing, was a call to man to witness what was about to occur.

Not only is there a voice of earth. Yonder the sun clothed himself in sackcloth for three hours, as much as to say: "There may be gloom for three days; the great Source of light hath veiled Himself, as in a mantle of night, for three days. As for three hours this darkness hangs, but as out of the darkness the light shines forth, so at the end of the three days shall the Sun of Righteousness shine out again, the great center of glory, with that glory which He had with the Father from the foundation of the world." It was the herald's voice that passed through the heavens, and that spoke through all the orbs of light, "Give attention, ye created beings, to what is to happen!" But it was not alone in the earth, which is the great center, nor in the heavens, which is the great source of light, that the tidings were proclaimed.

Look in yonder valley. The tombs are there; the prophets have been buried there. Yon hillside is full of the resting-places of the dead; generations on generations have been buried there; friends are walking in it, and they are saying, "Yonder is a mighty judge in Israel; there is the tomb of a prophet." They were passing to and fro through that valley of death when the earthquake's tread was heard, and behold! the tombs were opened, the graves displayed the dead within, and there was a voice that seemed to call from the very depths of the graves, "Hear, O sons of men!"

What feelings must have thrilled through the hearts of those who stood by those monuments and bended over those graves, when, thrown wide open, the doors bursting, and the rocks giving way, they saw the forms of death come forth and recognized friends that once they had known. What was to occur? What could all this mean? Then the great sacrifice was offered. It was three o'clock in the afternoon when Christ was to give up the ghost. Yonder the multitude of pious people were gathered toward the temple. The outer court was full; the doors and gates which lead into the sanctuary were crowded; the lamb was before the altar; the priest in his vestments had taken the sacrificial knife; the blood was to be shed at the hour of three; the multitude were looking.

Yonder hangs a veil; it hides that inner sanctuary; there are cherubim in yonder with their wings spread over the mercy-seat; the shekinah once dwelt there; God Himself in His glory was there and the people are bending to look in. No one enters into that veil save the high priest, and he, with blood and in the midst of incense, but once a year; but it was the mercy-seat and the eye of every pious Jew was directed toward that veil, thinking of the greater glory which lay beyond it.

As the hour of three came and as the priest was taking the sacrificial knife from the altar and was about to slay the lamb, behold! an unseen hand takes hold of that veil and tears it apart from top to bottom, and has thrown open the mercy-seat, not before seen by men. The cherubim are there; the altar with its covering of blood is there; the resting-place of the ark is there; it is the holiest of holies. Methinks the priest drops the knife, the lamb goes free, for the Lamb that was slain from the foundation of the world is suffering for man. The way to the holy of holies is open,—a new and living way, which men may not close, which priest alone can not enter; but a way is open whereby humanity, opprest and downtrodden, from all parts of the earth, may find its way to the mercy-seat of God. There was a call to the pious worshiper by voices which seemed to say: "An end to all the sacrifices, an end to all the suffering victims, an end to all the sprinkled hyssop that is used in purification, for One has come to do the will of God on whom the burden of man had been laid."

Now here were all these calls to humanity from all parts, as if to announce the great transaction. While all this was occurring Christ was on the cross, suffering the agony of crucifixion. How deep that agony we need not attempt to tell you; it was fearful; and yet no complaint escaped His lips, no murmuring was there. He bore the sins of many in His own flesh on the tree. He heard the multitudes revile Him; He saw them wag their heads; He remembered that the disciples had fled from Him—one followed afar off, but the rest had gone; and yet He complained not. Friends and kindred had all left Him and He trod the wine-press alone. He drank the cup in all its bitterness and no complaint escaped from Him. One left Him that had never forsaken Him before. "The world is gone, the disciples I have fed and taught have all fled and passed away,—all have forsaken Me."

But there was no time until that moment of fearful darkness came, when all the load of guilt was upon Him and for our sins He was smitten, that His spirit was crusht, and He called out, "My God, my God, why hast thou forsaken me?" All else might go—it were little; "Why hast thou forsaken me?" But it is over; the darkness is past; the load is borne; and I hear Him say, "It is finished"; He bows His head and dies.

Now there is publicity for the transaction. It demanded public investigation, it received it. There was not only the mental agony united with the agony of crucifixion, but there was the voluntary giving up of His life; yet, lest there might be some suspicion, to all this was added the proof of the fact of His death. When the limbs of the others were broken and He was perceived to be dead, the soldier thrust the spear into His side and there came out of that side both water and blood.

There is a peculiarity in the sacred writings. A little incident that seems to be mentioned without care becomes the strongest possible proof, not only of the fact of Christ's death, but of the nature of His death. When that sentence was written the human frame was not understood, the circulation of the blood was not understood. Anatomists had not then, as they have now, unveiled the human system; the great science of pathology had not yet been clearly taught to man; and yet in that sentence we have almost a world of meaning. For it is well attested now that where persons die from violent mental emotion, by what is termed a broken heart, a crusht spirit, there is always formed a watery secretion around the heart. It was not known then to the soldier who lifted up the spear and pierced the body; but so much of that water had secreted around the heart that he saw it issuing forth from the pierced side, unstained by blood, which showed that the great heart had been crusht by agony within.

When taken from the cross He was put in the sepulcher. His friends had given Him up, His disciples had forsaken Him; some of them saw Him die; they knew that He was crucified and they abandoned Him. They were returning to their former employments; but His enemies remembered He had said He would rise the third day, and they put a guard around Him. The Roman soldiers were there; the king's seal was on the stone rolled over the mouth of the sepulcher; they made everything secure. Here again God ordered that we should have abundant proof of Christ's crucifixion.

He was crucified on Friday, which was to them the last day of the week, resting in the grave on our Saturday, which is their Sabbath, and then comes the first day of the week, our Sabbath morning, made our Sabbath because of Christ's resurrection from the dead. There came an humble visitant to the tomb,

Mary Magdalene; she had been healed of much, forgiven much and she loved Him. Mary, the mother of James, came also and beheld the scenes that occurred; but there had been strange commotions elsewhere.

Heaven had been gathering around that grave. Angels had been watching there; they had seen the Roman guard; they had seen the shining spear and polished shield; they had seen that Christ was held as a prisoner by the greatest powers on earth. Methinks I see the angelic host as they gathered round the throne of God and looked up into the face of Omnipotence, and if ever there was a time when there was silence in heaven for half an hour, it was before the morning light of the third day dawned. I hear them say "How long shall man triumph? How long shall human power exalt itself? How long shall the powers of darkness hold jubilee? Let us away and roll away the stone; let us away and frighten yonder Roman guard and drive them from the sepulcher."

They waited until permission was given. I see the angel coming down from the opening doors of glory; he hastens outside the walls of Jerusalem and down to the sepulcher; when they saw him coming the keepers shook, they became like dead men; he rolls away the stone and sets himself by the mouth of the sepulcher. Christ, girding Himself with all the power of His divinity, rises from the grave. He leads captivity captive, tears the crown from the head of death, and makes light the darkness of the grave. Behold Him as He rises just preparatory to His rising up to glory. Oh, what a moment was that! Hell was preparing for its jubilee; the powers of earth were preparing for a triumph; but as the grave yields its prey, Christ, charged with being an impostor, is proved to be the Son of God with power; it is the power of His resurrection from the dead.

There was Christ's resurrection from the dead. He became the first fruits of them that slept. But to give the amplest proofs of His resurrection He lingered on earth to be seen of men, and to be seen in such a manner as to show that He was still the Savior

Christ. In my younger days I used to often wonder why was it that Mary Magdalene came first to the sepulcher, and the mother of James that stood there—why He should appear to them; but in later days I have said it was to show that He was the Savior still; that the same nature was there which had made Him stoop to the lowliest of the low—the power that enabled Him to heal the guiltiest of the guilty; that that power, that compassion, were with Him still.

Tho now raised beyond death and triumphing over hell, He still had within Him the Savior's heart. Methinks I see, when Peter had run in anxiety to tell the news, Mary remained there; she could not fully comprehend it; the grave was open, the napkins were there; it was said He was not there, but He was risen. And yet, there was a darkness upon her; she could not fully conceive, it seems to me, the resurrection of the dead. She stood wondering, when she heard a voice behind her which said, "Woman, why weepest thou?" Bathed in tears as she was, she turned round and saw the man standing, and taking him to be the gardener, and supposing that he had taken the body and carried it away as not fit to lie in that tomb or be in that garden, she said: "If thou hast taken, him away, tell me where thou hast laid him, and I will take him away." If He must not lie in this tomb, if He can not lie in the garden, if as a malefactor He must be cast out from man, tell me where the body is and I will take it away. It was a proof of her affection.

A voice said, "Mary, Mary." Oh, she recognized it, and her heart cried out: "Rabboni, my Lord and my God!" and then she would have thrown herself at His feet and bathed those feet again with her tears, but He said, "Touch me not, I am not ascended to my Father; go and tell the disciples and Peter that I am risen from the dead." See the compassion of the Savior! and then that message! "Tell the disciples and Peter." Why send a message to him? Because he curst and swore and denied the Master. The other disciples might have said, "If Christ is risen, He may receive and bless us all; but Peter is gone, hopelessly and irretrievably gone; he that forsook his Master and denied Him, there is no hope for him." And yet said Jesus, "Go and tell the disciples and Peter"—poor backslidden Peter.

Jesus knew his sorrow and anguish and almost felt the throbbings of his broken heart, and He sent a message to Peter. He may be a disciple still—may come back and be saved through the boundless love of Christ. Oh, the compassion of the Son of God! Thank God that Peter's Savior is on the throne this morning!

Not only was He seen by these, but He met with the disciples journeying by the way and explained the Scriptures to them; and as they met in the upper room He was there. When the doors were unopened He came in their midst and said, "Peace!" breathed on them and said, "Receive ye the Holy Ghost." Thus He met with them and said to Thomas, "Reach hither thy fingers, and be not faithless but believing."

Then afterward He was seen by five hundred, and from the Mount of Olives, while the disciples were gathered around Him, He was received up into glory. They saw Him and as He went He blest them. The last vision that ever humanity had of the Son of God ere he ascended to heaven was that of spreading out His hands in blessing. Oh, my Savior hath thus gone up, and He dropt from those outstretched hands a blessing which falls to-day like the gentle dew all over the earth; it reaches heart after heart. It hath reached patriarchs, apostles, martyrs, fathers, and mothers and little children, and, thank God, the heavenly dew, as from those outstretched hands, is coming down on our assembly this very morning. On this glad day blessings are dropping from the throne of God upon us from this risen Savior. He hath ascended up on high, the gates have opened for Him, and He hath gone to His throne in glory.

Let us look at a few of the results that flow to us from these facts thus sustained of His death and resurrection from the dead!

In the first place it established all Bible declarations. It had been predicted that He should not stay in the grave, and when He arose it put the seal to the Old Testament as the Word of

God. The prophecy in Him fulfilled gave glorious proof that the other parts of it should be also fulfilled as the word of an unchanging God.

Again, in His resurrection we see a proof of His divine power. No man hath been raised from the dead by his own power. All died, from Adam to Moses, with the exception of Enoch and Elijah, who, because of their devotion and acknowledgment of the divine head, themselves became prophets of a coming Savior. He rose by His own power. He conquered death itself, the grave, and the whole powers of humanity.

Jupiter is represented by an old classic writer as saying to the lesser gods that if all of them combined together and should endeavor to throw down his throne—if all power was arrayed against him—he, by his own might, would be able to overcome them all. What was fiction with the ancients becomes gloriously realized in Christ. Take all the powers of humanity—the Jewish power, the Roman power; the power of learning, of art, of public opinion; take all the powers of earth and hell, death and the grave, and combine them all against the Savior and, without one effort, without one single apparent movement—the Sleeper lies in death, His eyes are sealed, and, as if all unconscious, for the warning had not been given before—in an instant those eyes were opened, that frame rises, the grave yields up its prey, death retires conquered, and Christ demonstrates Himself to be the ruler of the whole universe. He made the earth to tremble, the sun to put on sackcloth, the very air to grow dark, the graves to open, the dead to come forth, and proclaimed Himself to be the conqueror of death and hell. So we have proof of His being the Son of God with power.

In that resurrection from the dead we have a pledge of our own resurrection. Christ has become the first-fruits of them that slept. You know the figure of the first-fruits as understood by the Jews. Their religion was connected with the seasons of the year—with the harvest crops; one of their feasts was called the feast of the first-fruits, and was on this wise: When the first heads of grain began to ripen in the field, and there was thus a pledge of harvest, they cut off those first ripened heads and went up to Jerusalem.

Before that the grain was not crusht, no bread was baked out of it, and nothing was done to appropriate that crop to man's use until those ripened heads of grain were brought up to Jerusalem and presented to the Lord as a thank-offering. He was acknowledged as Lord of the harvest and they were laid up as a kind of thank-offering before God. They were the first-fruits. Then they went away to the fields and all through Judea the sickle was thrust in, the grain was reaped and gathered into sheaves, and when the harvest was secured they baked the bread for their children out of this first grain. They came up to the temple, where the first-fruits had been laid, and they held a feast of thanksgiving and shouted harvest home. The old harvest feast seems to be descended from this ancient custom.

Christ rose as the first-fruits, and there is to be a glorious resurrection. Christ came, the first man to rise in this respect, by His own power, from the grave, having snatched the crown from death, having thrown light into the grave, having Himself ascended up toward glory. He goes up in the midst of the shouts of angels; the heavens open before Him; yonder is the altar; there is the throne, and around it stand the seraphim and the cherubim; and Christ enters, the victor, and sits down upon the throne, from henceforth expecting until His enemies be made His footstool. He is the first-fruits of the harvest, but the angels are to be sent out like the reapers, and by and by humanity is coming.

As Christ, the first-fruits, passed through the grave and went up to glory, so there shall come forth from their sleeping dust in Asia, in Africa, in Europe, and in America, from every mountain top, from the depths of the sea, from deep ravines, and from plains outspread—oh, there shall come in the time of the glorious harvest—the uprising of humanity, when all the nations, waking from their long sleep, shall rise and shall shout the harvest home! Thank God! At that time none shall be wanting.

Oh, they come, they come, from the nations of the past and from the generations yet unborn! I see the crowd gathering there. Behold the angels are waiting, and as the hosts rise from the dead they gather round the throne. Christ invites His followers to overcome and sit down with Him on His throne, as He overcame and sat down with the Father on His throne. In that is the pledge of our resurrection from the dead. Can I not suffer, since Christ suffered? Can I not die, since Christ died? Let the grave be my resting-place, for Christ rested there. Is it cold? The warmth of His animation is in it. He shall be beside me in all His spirit's power. Does the load of earth above me and beneath which I am placed press upon me? Christ hath power to burst the tomb, tho deep it be, and I shall rise through His almighty power.

Yet, let the malice of men be directed against me; let me be taken, if it must be, as a martyr and be bound to the stake; let the fagots be kindled, let the flame ascend, let my body be burned; gather my ashes, grind my bones to powder, scatter them on the ocean's surface; or carry those ashes to the top of yonder volcano and throw them within its consuming fire—let them be given to the dust—and yet I can sing:

"God my Redeemer lives,And ever from the skiesLooks down and watches all my dust,Till He shall bid it rise."

Thank God! it may be scattered on the wings of the wind— Christ is everywhere present; He has marked every particle and it shall rise again by His own almighty power. And what is it to sleep awhile if I am Christ's? To die, if I am like Christ in dying? and be buried, if I am like Christ in being buried? I trust I shall be like Him when He comes forth in His glory. I shall be like Him, for the apostle says, "We shall be like him, for we shall see him as he is"; "We shall be changed from glory into glory, into the same image as by the Spirit of God."

It would be a great change to be changed from glory to glory, from saints to angels, from angels to cherubim, from cherubim to seraphim, from glory to glory; but, thank God! we shall not stop being changed; for the change shall go on from glory to glory until we shall be transformed into the likeness of the Son of God, brighter than angels ever shone, more glorious than were ever cherubim.

We shall be near the throne; we shall sit beside Him, for He hath made room for us there. Then, if we can calmly look at death and face him, because his strength has been overcome, it reconciles us to parting a little while with friends. A father or a mother may be taken from us, but we shall see them again; they shall not sleep forever. The little ones that drop from our arms, we can almost see them this morning; some of us can almost feel them in our arms—can see the glance of that beautiful eye and hear the sound of that little prattling lip; they seem to be with us now, as a little while ago they dropt from out of our arms. We followed them to the grave and left them there, where the winter's storm has been howling around them.

Sometimes loneliness like that terrible storm has swept over our hearts and left them almost in despair; but through Christ's resurrection we see our children yonder in glory, safe in the Savior's arms. Their little forms shall rise all-glorious from the tomb in the morning of the resurrection; we shall find them, for Jesus is the resurrection and the life.

All this comes to us from the resurrection of Christ from the dead. He died once; He dies no more; the condemnation of death is forever gone; He sits on the throne of everlasting dominion; His kingdom is an eternal kingdom; and as He died once and has risen to die no more, so when we have died once and gone to the grave and entered the dark valley and shadow of death, and we come up safely on the other side, thank God! death is passed forever; we shall then put our feet on the neck of the monster and shall be able to say:

"Oh death, where is thy sting? Oh grave, where is thy victory?"

Looking at the resurrection of Christ we exclaim, Thanks be unto God who hath given us the victory! Such is the eternity and blessedness that awaits us. Thank God for a spiritual body! Here some of us long to triumph over nature. We would grasp, if we could, angelic wisdom; but our brows will ache with pain, our frames decay, our eyes grow dim, our hearing fail. This flesh of ours will not stand hours of painful study and seasons of protracted labor; but, thank God! when the body that now oppresses us is laid in the grave a spiritual body will be given to us, pure, ethereal, and holy. Oh, what an extent of knowledge shall flash upon us; what light and glory; what spirituality and power! Then we shall not need to ask an angel anything. We shall know as we are known. Jesus will be our teacher; the Everlasting God, the Man whose name is Wonderful, the Counselor, the Prince of Peace. He Himself shall be our Leader. We shall know then as also we are known.

Then rejoice in God. Dry up those tears. Cast away that downcast look. Child of the dust, you are an heir of glory. There is a crown all burnished for you; there is a mansion all ready for you; there is a white robe prepared for you; there is eternal glory for you; angels are to be your servants and you are to reign with the King of Kings forever. But while you wait on earth, be witnesses for God; attest the glory of your Master; rise in the greatness of His strength; bind sin captive to your chariot wheels; go onward in your heavenly career, and be as pure as your ascended Head is pure. Be active in works of mercy; be angels of light; be names of fire; go on your mission of mercy and convert the world unto God before you go up higher. When you go, not only go forward to present yourself, but may every one of you be able to say: "Here am I and those which Thou hast given me."

THEODORE PARKER

THE TRANSIENT
AND PERMANENT IN CHRISTIANITY

BIOGRAPHICAL NOTE

Theodore Parker, American divine and reformer, was born at Lexington, Mass., in 1810. He was educated at Harvard and graduated from the Divinity School of that University in 1836. The following year he was ordained pastor of Roxbury Christian Church, and first attracted attention by his sermon on the "Transient and Permanent in Christianity," preached in 1841. This sermon was ultimately the cause of his practical exclusion from the Unitarian body, and in 1846 he became minister to the Twenty-eighth Congregational Society in Boston.

In this pastorate he became well known to all denominations from the remarkable sermons he preached for seven years in Music Hall. He died of consumption at Florence, Italy, in 1860. His powerful intellect and vigorous eloquence were exhibited in the many controversial sermons he preached, both as a believer in the nonsupernaturalism of present Christianity and as a practical humanitarian. He figured as one of the leading abolitionists of New England.

THEODORE PARKER

1810-1860
THE TRANSIENT
AND PERMANENT IN CHRISTIANITY

Heaven and earth shall pass away; but my words shall not pass away.—Luke xxi., 33.

In this sentence we have a very clear indication that Jesus of Nazareth believed the religion He taught would be eternal, that the substance of it would last forever. Yet there are some who are affrighted by the faintest rustle which a heretic makes among the dry leaves of theology; they tremble lest Christianity itself should perish without hope. Ever and anon the cry is raised, "The Philistines be upon us, and Christianity is in danger." The least doubt respecting the popular theology, or the existing machinery of the Church; the least sign of distrust in the religion of the pulpit, or the religion of the street, is by some good men supposed to be at enmity with faith in Christ, and capable of shaking Christianity itself. On the other hand, a few bad men, and a few pious men, it is said, on both sides of the water, tell us the day of Christianity is past. The latter, it is alleged, would persuade us that hereafter piety must take a new form; the teachings of Jesus are to be passed by; that religion is to wing her way sublime, above the flight of Christianity, far away, toward heaven, as the fledged eaglet leaves forever the nest which sheltered his callow youth. Let us therefore devote a few moments to this subject, and consider what is transient in Christianity, and what is permanent therein.

In actual Christianity,—that is, in that portion of Christianity which is preached and believed,—there seems to have been, ever since the time of its earthly Founder, two elements, the one transient, the other permanent. The one is the thought, the folly, the uncertain wisdom, the theological notions, the impiety of man; the other, the eternal truth of God. These two bear, perhaps, the same relation to each other that the phenomena of outward nature, such as sunshine and cloud, growth, decay and reproduction, bear to the great law of nature, which underlies and supports them all. As in that case more attention is commonly paid to the particular phenomena than to the general law, so in this case more is generally given to the transient in Christianity than to the permanent therein.

It must be confest, tho with sorrow, that transient things form a great part of what is commonly taught as religion. An undue place has often been assigned to forms and doctrines, while too little stress has been laid on the divine life of the soul, love to God, and love to man. Religious forms may be useful and beautiful. They are so, whenever they speak to the soul, and answer a want thereof. In our present state some forms are perhaps necessary. But they are only the accident of Christianity, not its substance. They are the robe, not the angel, who may take another robe quite as becoming and useful. One sect has many forms; another, none. Yet both may be equally Christian, in spite of the redundance or the deficiency. They are a part of the language in which religion speaks, and exist, with few exceptions, wherever man is found. In our calculating nation, in our rationalizing sect, we have retained but two of the rites so numerous in the early Christian Church, and even these we have attenuated to the last degree, leaving them little more than a specter of the ancient form. Another age may continue or forsake both; may revive old forms, or invent new ones to suit the altered circumstances of the times, and yet be Christians quite as good as we, or our fathers of the dark ages. Whether the apostles designed these rites to be perpetual seems a question which belongs to scholars and antiquarians,—not to us, as Christian men and women. So long as they satisfy or help the pious heart, so long they are good. Looking behind or around us, we see that the forms and rites of the Christians are quite as fluctuating as those of the heathens, from whom some of them have been, not unwisely, adopted by the earlier Church.

Any one, who traces the history of what is called Christianity, will see that nothing changes more from age to age than the doctrines taught as Christian, and insisted on as essential to Christianity and personal salvation. What is falsehood in one province passes for truth in another. The heresy of one age is the orthodox belief and "only infallible rule" of the next. Now Arius, and now Athanasius, is lord of the ascendant. Both were excommunicated in their turn, each for affirming what the other denied. Men are burned for professing what men are burned for denying. For centuries the doctrines of the Christians were no better, to say the least, than those of their contemporary pagans. The theological doctrines derived from our fathers seem to have come from Judaism, heathenism, and the caprice of philosophers, far more than they have come from the principle and sentiment of Christianity. The doctrine of the Trinity, the very Achilles of theological dogmas, belongs to philosophy and not religion; its subtleties cannot even be expressed in our tongue. As old religions became superannuated, and died out, they left to the rising faith, as to a residuary legatee, their forms and their doctrines; or rather, as the giant in the fable left his poisoned garment to work the overthrow of his conqueror. Many tenets that pass current in our theology seem to be the refuse of idol temples, the offscourings of Jewish and heathen cities rather than the sands of virgin gold which the stream of Christianity has worn off from the rock of ages, and brought in its bosom for us. It is wood, hay, and stubble, wherewith men have built on the corner-stone Christ laid. What wonder the fabric is in peril when tried by fire? The stream of Christianity, as men receive it, has caught a stain from every soil it has filtered through, so that now it is not the pure water from the well of life which is offered to our lips, but streams troubled and polluted by man with mire and dirt. If Paul and Jesus could read our books of theological doctrines, would they accept as their teaching what men have vented in their name? Never, till the letters of Paul had faded out of his memory, never, till the words of Jesus had been torn out from the book of life. It is their notions about Christianity men have taught as the only living word of God. They have piled their own rubbish against the temple of truth where piety comes up to worship; what wonder the pile seems unshapely and like to fall? But these theological doctrines are fleeting as the leaves on the trees. They—

"Are foundNow green in youth, now withered on the ground;Another race the following spring supplies;They fall successive, and successive rise."

Like the clouds of the sky, they are here to-day; to-morrow, all swept off and vanished; while Christianity itself, like the heaven above, with its sun, and moon, and uncounted stars, is always over our head, tho the cloud sometimes debars us of the needed light. It must of necessity be the case that our reasonings, and therefore our theological doctrines, are imperfect, and so perishing. It is only gradually that we approach to the true system of nature by observation and reasoning, and work out our philosophy and theology by the toil of the brain. But meantime, if we are faithful, the great truths of mortality and religion, the deep sentiment of love to man and love to God, are perceived intuitively, and by instinct, as it were, tho our theology be imperfect and miserable. The theological notions of Abraham, to take the story as it stands, were exceedingly gross, yet a greater than Abraham has told us, "Abraham desired to see my day, saw it, and was glad." Since these notions are so fleeting, why need we accept the commandment of men as the doctrine of God?

This transitoriness of doctrines appears in many instances, of which two may be selected for a more attentive consideration.

First, the doctrine respecting the origin and authority of the Old and New Testaments. There has been a time when men were burned for asserting doctrines of natural philosophy which rested on evidence the most incontestable, because those doctrines conflicted with sentences in the Old Testament. Every word of that Jewish record was regarded as miraculously inspired, and therefore as infallibly true. It was believed that the Christian religion itself rested thereon, and must stand or fall with the immaculate Hebrew text. He was deemed no small sinner who found mistakes in the manuscripts. On the authority of the written word man was taught to believe impossible legends, conflicting assertions; to take fiction for fact, a dream for a miraculous revelation of God, an Oriental poem for a grave history of miraculous events, a collection of amatory idyls for a serious discourse "touching the mutual love of Christ and the Church"; they have been taught to accept a picture sketched by some glowing Eastern imagination, never intended to be taken for a reality, as a proof that the infinite God spoke in human words, appeared in the shape of a cloud, a flaming bush, or a man who ate, and drank, and vanished into smoke; that He gave counsels to-day, and the opposite to-morrow; that He violated His own laws, was angry, and was only dissuaded by a mortal man from destroying at once a whole nation,—millions of men who rebelled against their leader in a moment of anguish. Questions in philosophy, questions in the Christian religion, have been settled by an appeal to that book. The inspiration of its authors has been assumed as infallible. Every fact in the early Jewish history has been taken as a type of some analogous fact in Christian history. The most distant events, even such as are still in the arms of time, were supposed to be clearly foreseen and foretold by pious Hebrews several centuries before Christ. It has been assumed at the outset, with no shadow of evidence, that those writers held a miraculous communication with God, such as He has granted to no other man. What was originally a presumption of bigoted Jews became an article of faith, which Christians were

119

burned for not believing. This has been for centuries the general opinion of the Christian Church, both Catholic and Protestant, tho the former never accepted the Bible as the only source of religious truth. It has been so. Still worse, it is now the general opinion of religious sects at this day. Hence the attempt, which always fails, to reconcile the philosophy of our times with the poems in Genesis writ a thousand years before Christ. Hence the attempt to conceal the contradictions in the record itself. Matters have come to such a pass that even now he is deemed an infidel, if not by implication an atheist, whose reverence for the Most High forbids him to believe that God commanded Abraham to sacrifice his son,—a thought at which the flesh creeps with horror; to believe it solely on the authority of an Oriental story, written down nobody knows when or by whom, or for what purpose; which may be a poem, but can not be the record of a fact, unless God is the author of confusion and a lie.

Now, this idolatry of the Old Testament has not always existed. Jesus says that none born of a woman is greater than John the Baptist, yet the least in the kingdom of heaven is greater than John. Paul tells us the law—the very crown of the old Hebrew revelation—is a shadow of good things which have now come; only a schoolmaster to bring us to Christ; and when faith has come, that we are no longer under the schoolmaster; that it was a law of sin and death, from which we are made free by the law of the spirit of life. Christian teachers themselves have differed so widely in their notion of the doctrines and meaning of those books that it makes one weep to think of the follies deduced therefrom. But modern criticism is fast breaking to pieces this idol which men have made out of the Scriptures. It has shown that here are the most different works thrown together; that their authors, wise as they sometimes were, pious as we feel often their spirit to have been, had only that inspiration which is common to other men equally pious and wise; that they were by no means infallible, but were mistaken in facts or in reasoning,—uttered predictions which time has not fulfilled; men who in some measure partook of the darkness and limited notions of their age, and were not always above its mistakes or its corruptions.

The history of opinions on the New Testament is quite similar. It has been assumed at the outset, it would seem with no sufficient reason, without the smallest pretense on its writers' part, that all of its authors were infallibly and miraculously inspired, so that they could commit no error of doctrine or fact. Men have been bid to close their eyes at the obvious difference between Luke and John, the serious disagreement between Paul and Peter; to believe, on the smallest evidence, accounts which shock the moral sense and revolt the reason, and tend to place Jesus in the same series with the Hercules and Appollonius of Tyana; accounts which Paul in the Epistles never mentions, tho he also had a vein of the miraculous running quite through him. Men have been told that all these things must be taken as part of Christianity, and if they accepted the religion, they must take all these accessories along with it; that the living spirit could not be had without the killing letter. All the books which caprice or accident had brought together between the lids of the Bible were declared to be the infallible Word of God, the only certain rule of religious faith and practise. Thus the Bible was made not a single channel, but the only certain rule of religious faith and practise. To disbelieve any of its statements, or even the common interpretation put upon those statements by the particular age or church in which the man belonged, was held to be infidelity, if not atheism. In the name of Him who forbids us to judge our brother, good men and pious men have applied these terms to others, good and pious as themselves. That state of things has by no means passed away. Men who cry down the absurdities of paganism in the worst spirit of the French "free thinkers" call others infidels and atheists, who point out, tho reverently, other absurdities which men have piled upon Christianity. So the world goes. An idolatrous regard for the imperfect scripture of God's word is the apple of Atalanta, which defeats theologians running for the hand of divine truth.

But the current notions respecting the infallible inspiration of the Bible have no foundation in the Bible itself. Which evangelist, which apostle of the New Testament, what prophet or psalmist of the Old Testament, ever claims infallible authority for himself or for others? Which of them does not in his own writings show that he was finite, and, with all his zeal and piety, possest but a limited inspiration, the bound whereof we can sometimes discover? Did Christ ever demand that men should assent to the doctrines of the Old Testament, credit its stories, and take its poems for histories, and believe equally two accounts that contradict one another? Has He ever told you that all the truths of His religion, all the beauty of a Christian life should be contained in the writings of those men who, even after His resurrection, expected Him to be a Jewish king; of men who were sometimes at variance with one another, and misunderstood His divine teachings? Would not those modest writers themselves be confounded at the idolatry we pay them? Opinions may change on these points, as they have often changed—changed greatly and for the worse since the days of Paul. They are changing now, and we may hope for the better; for God makes man's folly as well his wrath to praise Him, and continually brings good out of evil.

Another instance of the transitoriness of doctrines taught as Christian is found in those which relate to the nature and authority of Christ. One ancient party has told us that He is the infinite God; another, that He is both God and man; a third, that He was a man, the son of Joseph and Mary, born as we are; tempted like ourselves; inspired as we may be, if we will pay the price. Each of the former parties believed its doctrine on this head was infallibly true, and formed the very substance of Christianity, and was one of the essential conditions of salvation, tho scarce any two distinguished teachers, of ancient or modern times, agree in their expression of this truth.

Almost every sect that has ever been, makes Christianity rest on the personal authority of Jesus, and not the immutable truth of the doctrines themselves, or the authority of God, who sent

Him into the world. Yet it seems difficult to conceive any reason why moral and religious truths should rest for their support on the personal authority of their revealer, any more than the truths of science on that of him who makes them known first or most clearly. It is hard to see why the great truths of Christianity rest on the personal authority of Jesus, more than the axioms of geometry rest on the personal authority of Euclid or Archimedes. The authority of Jesus as of all teachers, one would naturally think, must rest on the truth of His words, and not their truth on His authority.

Opinions respecting the nature of Christ seem to be constantly changing. In the three first centuries after Christ, it appears, great latitude of speculation prevailed. Some said He was God, with nothing of human nature, His body only an illusion; others that He was man, with nothing of the divine nature, His miraculous birth having no foundation in fact. In a few centuries it was decreed by councils that He was God, thus honoring the divine element; next, that He was man also, thus admitting the human side. For some ages the Catholic Church seems to have dwelt chiefly on the divine nature that was in Him, leaving the human element to mystics and other heretical persons, whose bodies served to flesh the swords of orthodox believers. The stream of Christianity has come to us in two channels,—one within the Church, the other without the Church,—and it is not hazarding too much to say that since the fourth century the true Christian life has been out of the established Church, and not in it, but rather in the ranks of dissenters. From the Reformation till the latter part of the last century, we are told, the Protestant Church dwelt chiefly on the human side of Christ, and since that time many works have been written to show how the two—perfect Deity and perfect manhood—were united in His character. But, all this time, scarce any two eminent teachers agree on these points, however orthodox they may be called. What a difference between the Christ of John Gerson and John Calvin,—yet were both accepted teachers and pious men. What a difference between the Christ of the Unitarians and the Methodists,—yet may men of both sects be true Christians and acceptable with God. What a difference between the Christ of Matthew and John,—yet both were disciples, and their influence is wide as Christendom and deep as the heart of man. But on this there is not time to enlarge.

Now, it seems clear that the notions men form about the origin and nature of the Scriptures, respecting the nature and authority of Christ, have nothing to do with Christianity except as its aids or its adversaries; they are not the foundation of its truths. These are theological questions, not religious questions. Their connection with Christianity appears accidental; for if Jesus had taught at Athens, and not at Jerusalem; if He had wrought no miracle, and none but the human nature had ever been ascribed to them; if the Old Testament had forever perished at His birth,—Christianity would still have been the word of God; it would have lost none of its truths. It would be just as true, just as beautiful, just as lasting, as now it is; tho we should have lost so many a blessed word, and the work of Christianity itself would have been, perhaps, a long time retarded.

To judge the future by the past, the former authority of the Old Testament can never return. Its present authority can not stand. It must be taken for what it is worth. The occasional folly and impiety of its authors must pass for no more than their value; while the religion, the wisdom, the love, which make fragrant its leaves, will still speak to the best hearts as hitherto, and in accents even more divine when reason is allowed her rights. The ancient belief in the infallible inspiration of each sentence of the New Testament is fast changing, very fast. One writer, not a skeptic, but a Christian of unquestioned piety, sweeps off the beginning of Matthew; another, of a different church and equally religious, the end of John. Numerous critics strike off several epistles. The Apocalypse itself is not spared, notwithstanding its concluding curse. Who shall tell us the work of retrenchment is to stop here; that others will not demonstrate what some pious hearts have long felt, that errors of doctrine and errors of fact may be found in many parts of the record, here and there, from the beginning of Matthew to the end of Acts? We see how opinions have changed ever since the apostles' time; and who shall assure us that they were not sometimes mistaken in historical as well as doctrinal matters; did not sometimes confound the actual with the imaginary; and that the fancy of these pious writers never stood in the place of their recollection?

But what if this should take place? Is Christianity then to perish out of the heart of the nations, and vanish from the memory of the world, like the religions that were before Abraham? It must be so, if it rest on a foundation which a scoffer may shake, and a score of pious critics shake down. But this is the foundation of a theology, not of Christianity. That does not rest on the decision of councils. It is not to stand or fall with the infallible inspiration of a few Jewish fishermen, who have writ their names in characters of light all over the world. It does not continue to stand through the forbearance of some critic, who can cut when he will the thread on which its life depends. Christianity does not rest on the infallible authority of the New Testament. It depends on this collection of books for the historical statement of its facts. In this we do not require infallible inspiration on the part of the writers, more than in the record of other historical facts. To me it seems as presumptuous, on the one hand, for the believer to claim this evidence for the truth of Christianity, as it is absurd, on the other hand, for the skeptic to demand such evidence to support these historical statements. I can not see that it depends on the personal authority of Jesus. He was the organ through which the Infinite spoke. It is God that was manifested in the flesh by Him, on whom rests the truth which Jesus brought to light, and made clear and beautiful in His life; and if Christianity be true, it seems useless to look for any other authority to uphold it, as for some one to support Almighty God. So if it could be proved—as it can not—in opposition to the greatest amount of historical evidence ever collected on any similar point, that the Gospels were the fabrication of designing and artful men, that

Jesus of Nazareth had never lived, still Christianity would stand firm, and fear no evil. None of the doctrines of that religion would fall to the ground; for, if true, they stand by themselves. But we should lose—oh, irreparable loss!—the example of that character, so beautiful, so divine, that no human genius could have conceived it, as none, after all the progress and refinement of eighteen centuries, seems fully to have comprehended its lustrous life. If Christianity were true, we should still think it was so, not because its record was written by infallible pens, nor because it was lived out by an infallible teacher; but that it is true, like the axioms of geometry, because it is true and is to be tried, by the oracle God places in the breast. If it rest on the personal authority of Jesus alone, then there is no certainty of its truth if He were ever mistaken in the smallest matter,—as some Christians have thought He was in predicting His second coming.

These doctrines respecting the Scriptures have often changed, and are but fleeting. Yet men lay much stress on them. Some cling to these notions as if they were Christianity itself. It is about these and similar points that theological battles are fought from age to age. Men sometimes use worst the choicest treasure which God bestows. This is especially true of the use men make of the Bible. Some men have regarded it as the heathen their idol, or the savage his fetish. They have subordinated reason, conscience, and religion to this. Thus have they lost half the treasure it bears in its bosom. No doubt the time will come when its true character shall be felt. Then it will be seen that, amid all the contradictions of the Old Testament,—its legends, so beautiful as fictions, so appalling as facts; amid its predictions that have never been fulfilled; amid the puerile conceptions of God which sometimes occur, and the cruel denunciations that disfigure both psalm and prophecy,—there is a reverence for man's nature, a sublime trust in God, and a depth of piety, rarely felt in these cold northern hearts of ours. Then the devotion of its authors, the loftiness of their aim, and the majesty of their life, will appear doubly fair, and prophet and psalmist will warm our hearts as never before. Their voice will cheer the young, and sanctify the gray-headed; will charm us in the toil of life, and sweeten the cup death gives us when he comes to shake off this mantle of flesh. Then will it be seen that the words of Jesus are the music of heaven sung in an earthly voice, and that the echo of these words in John and Paul owe their efficacy to their truth and their depth, and to no accidental matter connected therewith. Then can the Word, which was in the beginning and now is, find access to the innermost heart of man, and speak there as now it seldom speaks. Then shall the Bible—which is a whole library of the deepest and most earnest thoughts and feelings, and piety, and love, ever recorded in human speech—be read oftener than ever before,—not with superstition, but with reason, conscience, and faith, fully active. Then shall it sustain men bowed down with many sorrows; rebuke sin, encourage virtue, sow the world broadcast and quick with the seed of love, that man may reap a harvest for life everlasting.

With all the obstacles men have thrown in its path, how much has the Bible done for mankind! No abuse has deprived us of all its blessings. You trace its path across the world from the day of Pentecost to this day. As a river springs up in the heart of a sandy continent, having its father in the skies, and its birthplace in distant unknown mountains; as the stream rolls on, enlarging itself, making in that arid waste a belt of verdure wherever it turns its way; creating palm groves and fertile plains, where the smoke of the cottager curls up at eventide, and marble cities send the gleam of their splendor far into the sky,—such has been the course of the Bible on the earth. Despite of idolaters bowing to the dust before it, it has made a deeper mark on the world than the rich and beautiful literature of all the heathen. The first book of the Old Testament tells man he is made in the image of God; the first of the New Testament gives us the motto, Be perfect as your Father in heaven. Higher words were never spoken. How the truths of the Bible have blest us! There is not a boy on all the hills of New England; not a girl born in the filthiest cellar which disgraces a capital in Europe, and cries to God against the barbarism of modern civilization; not a boy nor a girl all Christendom through, but their lot is made better by that great book.

Doubtless the time will come when men shall see Christ also as He is. Well might He still say, "Have I been so long with you, and yet hast thou not known me?" No! we have made Him an idol, have bowed the knee before Him, saying, "Hail, king of the Jews!" called Him "Lord, Lord!" but done not the things which He said. The history of the Christian world might well be summed up in one word of the evangelist—"and there they crucified him"; for there has never been an age when the men did not crucify the Son of God afresh. But if error prevail for a time and grow old in the world, truth will triumph at the last, and then we shall see the Son of God as He is. Lifted up, He shall draw all nations unto Him. Then will men understand the word of Jesus, which shall not pass away. Then shall we see and love the divine life that He lived. How vast has His influence been! How His spirit wrought in the hearts of His disciples, rude, selfish, bigoted, as at first they were! How it has wrought in the world! His words judge the nations. The wisest son of man has not measured their height. They speak to what is deepest in profound men, what is holiest in good men, what is divinest in religious men. They kindle anew the flame of devotion in hearts long cold. They are spirit and life. His truth was not derived from Moses and Solomon; but the light of God shone through Him, not colored, not bent aside. His life is the perpetual rebuke of all time since. It condemns ancient civilization; it condemns modern civilization. Wise men we have since had, and good men; but this Galilean youth strode before the whole world thousands of years, so much of divinity was in Him. His words solve the question of this present age. In Him the Godlike and the human met and embraced, and a divine life was born. Measure Him by the world's greatest sons—how poor they are! Try Him by the best of men—how little and low they appear! Exalt Him as much as we may, we shall yet perhaps come short of the mark. But still was He not our brother; the son of man, as we are; the son of God, like ourselves? His excellence—was it not human excellence? His wisdom, love, piety,—sweet and celestial as they were,—are they not what we also may attain? In Him, as in a mirror, we may see the image of God, and go on from glory to glory, till we are changed into the same image, led by the spirit which enlightens the humble. Viewed in this way, how beautiful is the life of Jesus! Heaven has come down to earth, or rather, earth has become heaven. The Son of God, come of age, has taken possession of His birthright. The brightest revelation is this of what is possible for all men,—if not now, at least hereafter. How pure is His spirit, and how encouraging its words! "Lowly sufferer," he seems to say, "see how I bore the cross. Patient laborer, be strong; see how I toiled for the unthankful and the merciless. Mistaken sinner, see of what thou art capable. Rise up, and be blest."

But if, as some early Christians began to do, you take a heathen view, and make Him a God, the Son of God in a peculiar and exclusive sense, much of the significance of His character is gone. His virtue has no merit, His love no feeling, His cross no burthen, His agony no pain. His death is an illusion, His resurrection but a show. For if He were not a man, but a god, what are all these things? What His words, His life, His excellence of achievement? It is all nothing, weighed against the illimitable greatness of Him who created the worlds and fills up all time and space! Then His resignation is no lesson, His life no model, His death no triumph to you or me, who are not gods, but mortal men, that know not what a day shall bring forth, and walk by faith "dim sounding on our perilous way." Alas! we have despaired of man, and so cut off his brightest hope.

In respect of doctrines as well as forms, we see all is transitory. "Everywhere is instability and insecurity." Opinions have changed most on points deemed most vital. Could we bring up a Christian teacher of any age, from the sixth to the fourteenth century, for example, tho a teacher of undoubted soundness of faith, whose word filled the churches of Christendom, clergymen would scarce allow him to kneel at their altar, or sit down with them at the Lord's table. His notions of Christianity could not be exprest in our forms, nor could our notions be made intelligible to his ears. The questions of his age, those on which Christianity was thought to depend,—questions which perplexed and divided the subtle doctors,—are no questions to us. The quarrels which then drove wise men mad now only excite a smile or a tear, as we are disposed to laugh or weep at the frailty of man. We have other straws of our own to quarrel for. Their ancient books of devotion do not speak to us; their theology is a vain word. To look back but a short period,—the theological speculations of our fathers during the last two centuries, their "practical divinity," even the sermons written by genius and piety are, with rare exceptions, found unreadable; such a change is there in the doctrines.

Now who shall tell us that the change is to stop here; that this sect or that, or even all sects united, have exhausted the river of life, and received it all in their canonized urns, so that we need draw no more out of the eternal well, but get refreshment nearer at hand? Who shall tell us that another age will not smile at our doctrines, disputes, and unchristian quarrels about Christianity, and make wide the mouth at men who walked brave in orthodox raiment, delighting to blacken the names of heretics, and repeat again the old charge, "He hath blasphemed"? Who shall tell us they will not weep at the folly of all such as fancied truth shone only into the contracted nook of their school, or sect, or coterie? Men of other times may look down equally on the heresy-hunters, and men hunted for heresy, and wonder at both. The men of all ages before us were quite as confident as we, that their opinion was truth, that their notion was Christianity and the whole thereof. The men who lit the fires of persecution, from the first martyr to Christian bigotry down to the last murder of the innocents, had no doubt their opinion was divine. The contest about transubstantiation and the immaculate purity of the Hebrew and Greek texts of the Scriptures was waged with bitterness unequaled in these days. The Protestant smiles at one, the Catholic at the other, and men of sense wonder at both. It might teach us all a lesson, at least of forbearance. No doubt an age will come in which ours shall be reckoned a period of darkness, like the sixth century,—when men groped for the wall, but stumbled and fell, because they trusted a transient notion, not an eternal truth; an age when temples were full of idols, set up by human folly; an age in which Christian light had scarce begun to shine into men's hearts. But while this change goes on, while one generation of opinions passes away, and another rises up, Christianity itself, that pure religion, which exists eternal in the constitution of the soul and the mind of God, is always the same. The Word that was before Abraham, in the very beginning, will not change, for that Word is truth. From this Jesus subtracted nothing; to this He added nothing. But He came to reveal it as the secret of God, that cunning men could not understand, but which filled the souls of men meek and lowly of heart. This truth we owe to God; the revelation thereof to Jesus, our elder brother, God's chosen son.

To turn away from the disputes of the Catholics and the Protestants, of the Unitarian and the Trinitarian, of old school and new school, and come to the plain words of Jesus of Nazareth,—Christianity is a simple thing, very simple. It is absolute, pure morality; absolute, pure religion,—the love of man; the love of God acting without let or hindrance. The only creed it lays down is the great truth which springs up spontaneous in the holy heart,—there is a God. Its watchword is, Be perfect as your Father in heaven. The only form it demands is a divine life,—doing the best thing in the best way, from the highest motives; perfect obedience to the great law of God. Its sanction is the voice of God in your heart; the perpetual presence of Him who made us and the stars over our head; Christ and the Father abiding within us. All this is very simple—a little child can understand it; very beautiful—the loftiest mind can find nothing so lovely. Try it by reason, conscience, and faith,—things highest in man's nature,—we see no redundance, we feel no deficiency. Examine the particular duties it enjoins,—humility, reverence, sobriety, gentleness, charity, forgiveness, fortitude, resignation, faith, and active love; try the whole extent of Christianity, so well summed up in the command, "Thou shalt love the Lord thy God with all thy heart, and with all thy soul, and with all thy mind; thou shalt love thy neighbor as thyself"; and is there anything therein that can perish? No, the very opponents of Christianity have rarely found fault with the teachings of Jesus. The end of Christianity seems to be to make all men one with God as Christ was one with Him; to bring them to such a state of obedience and goodness that we shall think divine thoughts and feel divine sentiments, and so keep the law of God by living a life of truth and love. Its means are purity and prayer; getting strength from God, and using it for our fellow-men as well as ourselves. It allows perfect freedom. It does not demand all men to think alike, but to think uprightly, and get as near as possible at truth; not all men to live alike, but to live holy, and get as near as possible to a life perfectly divine. Christ set up no Pillars of Hercules, beyond which men must not sail the sea in quest of truth. He says, "I have many things to say unto you, but ye cannot bear them now.... Greater works than these shall ye do." Christianity lays no rude hand on the sacred peculiarity of individual genius and character. But there is no Christian sect which does not fetter a man. It would make all men think alike, or smother their conviction in silence. Were all men Quakers or Catholics, Unitarians or Baptists, there would be much less diversity of thought, character, and life, less of truth active in the world, than now. But Christianity gives us the largest liberty of the sons of God; and were all men Christians after the fashion of Jesus, this variety would be a thousand times greater than now; for Christianity is not a system of doctrines, but rather a method of attaining oneness with God. It demands, therefore, a good life of piety within, of purity without, and gives the promise that whoso does God's will shall know of God's doctrine.

MACLEOD

THE TRUE CHRISTIAN MINISTRY

BIOGRAPHICAL NOTE

Norman Macleod, the eminent Scotch preacher, was born at Campbeltown, in Argyleshire, in 1812. In his preaching he departed from the rigid conventionality of the Scottish Church. His large vision and broad culture gave unusual distinction both to his writings and to his pulpit oratory. He was conspicuous for philanthropic efforts, and frequently held evening services for workingmen. He distinguished himself by his popular Christian writing and by his pulpit oratory. He was practical and manly, of godly nature, with extreme adaptability, and greatly esteemed by Queen Victoria, who made him her chaplain in 1857. He died in 1872.

MACLEOD

1812-1872
THE TRUE CHRISTIAN MINISTRY[2]

Neither pray I for these alone, but for them also which shall believe on me through their word;

That they all may be one; as thou, Father, art in me, and I in thee, that they also may be one in us; that the world may believe that thou hast sent me.—John xvii., 20, 21.

"These words spake Jesus, and lifted up his eyes to heaven, and said, Father, the hour is come!" The hour was indeed come for which the whole world had been in travail since creation, and which was for ever to mark a new era in the history of the universe. The hour was come when, having finished the work given Him to do, He was to return to His Father, but only after ending His earthly journey along the awful path on which He was now entering, and which led through Gethsemane, the cross, and the grave. At such a moment in His life He lifted up His eyes in perfect peace, from the sinful and sorrowful world, to the heavens glorious in their harmony and soothing in their silence, and said, "Father!" One feels a solemn awe, as if entering the holy of holies, in seeking to enter into the mind of Christ as exprest in this prayer. Never were such words spoken on earth, never were such words heard in heaven. I ask no other evidence to satisfy my spirit that they are the truth of God than the evidence of their

---

2   Printed here by permission of the publishers, Messrs. Wm. Blackwood & Sons.

own light, revealing as it does the speaker as being Himself light and life, who verily came from God and went to God.

But let me in all reverence endeavor to express a few thoughts, as to the general meaning of this prayer, with reference more especially to that portion of it which I have selected as the subject of my discourse.

The one all-absorbing desire of our Lord, as here exprest—the ultimate end sought to be realized by Him—is that God might be glorified as a Father, and that by the world seeing His love revealed in sending His Son into the world to save sinners. "God is love," but "In this was manifested the love of God toward us, because that God sent his only-begotten Son into the world that we might live through him"—a love which, when spiritually seen and possest by us, is itself life eternal; for "This is life eternal that they might know thee, the only true God, and Jesus Christ, whom thou hast sent;" but "He that loveth not, knoweth not God; for God is love."

All "religion" accordingly, all good, all righteousness, peace, joy, glory, to man and to the universe, are bound up in this one thing, knowing God as a Father. Out of this right condition of love to God, must necessarily come our right condition towards man, that of love to man as a brother with special love, the love of character, to Christian brethren. Such a religion as this was never possest as an idea even by the greatest thinkers among the civilized heathen nations; far less was it realized by any. Whatever knowledge many had about God, they knew Him not as a Father to be loved and trusted, and therefore obeyed. When St. Paul addrest the Athenians, he could find such a thought exprest by a poet only, who had said, "We are also His offspring." It is only in the line of supernatural revelation of God to man, as given to and received by Abraham, "the friend," and perfected by Christ the Son, that this knowledge of God has been possest by man. But even among those to whom this true revelation was given about God, how few truly knew Him!

The want of this religion, whatever else might exist that was called by that name, was the complaint made by God against His people of old, "They do not know me!" "They proceed from evil to evil," He cries, for "they know not me, saith the Lord." "Through deceit they refuse to know me, saith the Lord;" and again: "Thus saith the Lord, Let not the wise man glory in his wisdom, neither let the mighty man glory in his might, let not the rich man glory in his riches; but let him that glorieth glory in this, that he understandeth and knoweth me, that I am the Lord which exercise loving-kindness, judgment, and righteousness, in the earth: for in these things I delight, saith the Lord." (Jer. ix., 23, 24.)

This was the sorrowing cry of Christ, "O righteous Father, the world hath not known thee!" This was His joy, "I have known thee, and these have known that thou hast sent me!"

But if Christ desired that His Father's name should be glorified, how was this to be accomplished? By what medium, or means? Now I would here observe that God's method of revealing Himself to man has ever been to do so by living men; and the Bible is a true record of such revelations in the past. Christianity is not the philosophy of life, but life itself; and is a revelation, not of abstract truth, but of the living personal God to living persons as His children, whom He hath created to glorify and enjoy Him for ever. The first grand medium of this revelation is the eternal Son of God. The very essence of God's character being love, He did not exist from all eternity with a mere capacity of loving, but without an object to love; like an eye capable of seeing light, but with no light to see. The object of His love was His Son, who from all eternity responded to that love and rejoiced in His Father. This eternal Son, when manifested in the flesh, revealed His Father directly, so that He could say, in all He was, and in all He did, and, in a true sense, in all He suffered, "He that hath seen me, hath seen the Father;" and men could say of Him, "We beheld His glory, the glory as of the only-begotten of the Father, full of grace and truth;" "The glory of God" was "in the face of Jesus Christ." Again, He had also, as the Son of Man, glorified His

137

Father; and, by His reverence for, confidence in, and obedience to, Him, and by His joy in Him, had indirectly revealed what he knew God to be to Him and to all as a Father. "I have glorified Thee on the earth: I have finished the work which Thou gavest me to do." Such was His finished work. But something more was yet to be accomplished. Ere He descends to Gethsemane, He desires anew to have the joy of revealing a Father's heart by revealing to the world His own heart of love as a Son to that Father. Hence His prayer, "Glorify thy Son, that thy Son also may glorify thee." He does not prescribe the new circumstances in which His long-tried and perfect filial confidence and love as a Son were to be manifested. With the absolute consecration of true sonship He leaves these circumstances to be determined by His Father. Now, as on the cross, He commits His spirit, as a little child, into His Father's hands. He desires only that in any way, by any means, He may have the joy of showing forth the reality, the endurance, and the triumph of His Sonship. His Father may fill His cup according to His own will, the Son will drink it. The Father may permit a crown of thorns to be placed on His brow, and every conceivable horror of great darkness from the hate of men and devils to be cast over Him like a funeral-pall; He may be rejected by all His brethren and by the Church and by the State—"Amen!" He cries. Let His body be broken and His blood shed, He will give thanks! One thing only He prays for, "Glorify thy Son, that thy Son also may glorify thee!" As a further end to be accomplished, He prays that He may have the joy of making others share the same divine love and joy, and therefore adds, "As thou hast given him power over all flesh, that he should give eternal life to as many as thou hast given him. And this is life eternal, that they might know thee, the only true God, and Jesus Christ, whom thou hast sent."

But while He as the Son was to be the first revealer of God the Father, He was not, therefore, to be the only revealer. He was the firstborn of many brethren in whom the same love was to be reproduced, and by whom the same high duty was to be performed. If the light of the glory of God shone directly in the face of Jesus Christ, that light was to be transmitted to those who were to shine as lights in the world, that others seeing them might glorify the same God. For now, as ever, God in a real sense manifests Himself in the flesh. Hence our Lord's desire that His brethren should, as sons, reveal the Father, like Himself the Son. He says accordingly, "As thou hast sent me into the world, even so have I also sent them into the world." Sent whom? Not apostles only, but those also who should believe through their word; not ministers of the Church only, but members also; all, in short, who were qualified to convince the world that God was a Father, by convincing it of this truth, that God had sent His Son to save sinners—the "faithful saying, worthy of all acceptation."

But the question is further suggested, What is this qualification? What is this which men must possess in order to accomplish Christ's purpose of inducing the world to believe? What is this evidence of Christianity which they are to present to the eyes of unbelieving men, by seeing which these are to know and glorify God as their Father in Christ? We reply, it is the oneness of those who are to be ambassadors from God and fellow-workers with Christ. "I pray for them," He says, and not for them only, but "for them also who shall believe on me through their word; that they all may be one; as thou, Father, art in me, and I in thee, that they may be one in us; that the world may believe that thou hast sent me."

Now this leads me to consider more particularly the nature of this oneness which is essential for such a successful mission as will convince the world of the truth of Christ's mission from the Father. What is meant by this oneness, or this union?

We are guided in our inquiry by three features which characterize it. First, It is a oneness such as subsists between Christ and God; secondly, It is a oneness which can be seen or appreciated; thirdly, It is a oneness which is calculated from its nature to convince the world of the truth of Christ's mission.

Now there are many kinds of union among men, which,

however wonderful or excellent, may be set aside as obviously not fulfilling these conditions, and not such, therefore, as Christ prayed for. There is, e. g., the unity of an army which marches as one man, implicitly obeying its commander even unto death and without a question. Yet, however grand this is, and however illustrative of the character of good soldiers of Jesus Christ, it does not fulfil the conditions specified. Nor does the wonderful unity of a State, which makes and imposes laws, proclaims war or peace, administers justice, and executes its judgments. In neither case is there any union such as subsists betwixt God and Christ; nor such as is in any sense adapted to convince the world that God has sent His Son to save sinners. The same may be alleged of any outward and visible unity of a body of men which might be called a Church. Its organization might be as wonderful, and its members as disciplined, and its power as remarkable, as those of an army; it might be held together like a state by its laws and its enactments, its rewards and punishments, and might energetically advance until it possest the dominion of the world, and attracted such attention as that all men might marvel at it; its members might assent to all the details of a creed however large; the same rights and ceremonies and modes of worship might be repeated throughout all its parts; and it might be able to continue its organized existence from age to age,—yet it would by no means follow that any such system, however remarkable, possest that inward spiritual unity desired in Christ's prayer, no more than the compact unity of Brahminism does, nor the still more extraordinary unity of Buddhism, with its temples, its priesthood, its creed, its rites and ceremonies, continuing unchanged during teeming centuries, and dominating over hundreds of millions of the human race. May not all these and many similar unities be fully and satisfactorily accounted for by principles in human nature, altogether irrespective of the fact of a supernatural power having come into the world to which their origin or continuance is owing? For there is a oneness in the churchyard as well as in the church. There might be a oneness of assent amongst a deaf multitude with regard to the beauty of music, because determined by the fiat of authority, but not as the result of hearing and of taste; and the same kind of oneness of judgment as to the beauty of pictures, on the part of those who were blind. Unity alone proves nothing, apart from its nature and its origin.

There is but one kind of unity or oneness which fulfils the specified conditions, and that is, oneness of character or of spiritual life—in one word, the oneness of love;—for this is the highest condition of a personal spirit. It is such love as God had and has to Christ; "That the love wherewith thou has loved me may be in them;" such love as the Son has to the Father, and such as He manifested to His disciples that very evening when, conscious of His divine glory, and "knowing that he was come from God, and went to God," He girded Himself with a towel and washed His disciples' feet. Hence the declaration, "The glory," that is, of character, "which thou gavest me I have given them, that they," through its possession, "may be one, even as we are one: I in them, and thou in me." Hence again His saying, "They are not of the world, even as I am not of the world;" and His prayer, "I pray not that thou shouldst take them out of the world, but that thou shouldst keep them from the evil." Such love as this, when in the soul of ordinary men, does not originate in their own hearts, however naturally benevolent or affectionate these may be. Our Lord in this prayer recognizes it as inseparable from faith in His own teaching, and from personal conviction of the truth which they themselves were to preach; for they had received His words, and had "known surely that I came out from thee, and they have believed that thou didst send me"; and so He prays, "Sanctify them through thy truth; thy word is truth."

Now, if we would divide, as with a prism, this pure light of love, we might discern it as being composed, as it were, of at least two colors, or features—first, love to God, exprest in the desire that He should be known; secondly, love to man, exprest in self-sacrifice that all should share this true love. But these

141

very features we discern as first existing in God the Father and in Christ the Son; for God desires, from the necessity of His own nature, that He should be known, and that all His rational creatures should see the glory of His character, and, in seeing it, should live. God has also manifested His love, according to the law of love, by giving and by self-sacrifice, inasmuch as He "spared not his own Son, but delivered him up for us all." In like manner, the Son desired that His Father might be known, and to accomplish this He became incarnate. He has manifested His love also in the form of self-sacrifice, in that His whole life and death were an offering up of Himself as a sacrifice unto God, and as an atonement for the sins of the world, in order that all men might be made partakers of His own eternal life in God. This, too, is the "mind" of the Holy Spirit, for He glorifies the Son, that the Son may glorify the Father, and glorifies Him in and by His true Church. Hence, wherever true love exists in man, it will manifest itself in these two forms; it will ever desire that God may be known, and will never "seek its own," but sacrifice itself that this end may be attained. In such oneness as this of mind, spirit, character—in one word, love—there is realized the first condition of that oneness for which our Lord prayed.

Secondly, This unity of character fulfils the second condition in its being such as the world can in some degree see and appreciate. Blind as the world is, it can see love in the form of self-sacrifice at least, seeking its good, even tho it may not at once see in this a revelation of such love as has its origin in the love of God to man. The world's heart can perceive more things and greater things than can its intellect. The child of the statesman or man of science may not be able to comprehend the world-politics of the one or the scientific discoveries of the other; but it can see and feel the love revealed in the glance of the eye, in the smile on the lips, or in the arms that clasp it to the bosom; and in seeing this, it sees an infinitely greater thing than the politics of the one or the scientific discoveries of the other. It sees, too, in this, tho unconsciously, the love of the Father's heart which fills the universe with glory, even as its eye, when opened to a little light, sees the same light which illumines a thousand worlds. And thus can the world see the light of love. Those who are in prison, in nakedness, or in thirst, are quite able to see and to appreciate the love that, for Christ's sake, visits them, clothes them, and gives them drink. The wretched lepers in the lazar-house, into which no one could enter and ever return to the world, could see and appreciate the love of the Moravian missionary who visited them, and who shut the door for ever between him and all he knew and loved, that he might share and alleviate the horrors of his wretched brethren whom he loved more than all. Blind as the world is, it can see this or nothing; bad as it is, it can appreciate this goodness or none.

Thirdly, Such a character is calculated also to convince the world that God has sent Christ to save sinners. Observe again what is our Lord's idea of the mission which was to convert the world; it is this, that those whom He sends, even as God had sent Himself, whether as apostles or as disciples, should give to their fellow men what they have first received from their living Head, Jesus Christ. They were to give "the words" which they received from Him, and which He had received from God—they were to give "the truth" which they received from Him, and which He Himself had glorified in His life and death, that God had sent Him to be the Savior of the world. They were also to manifest that life which they had received from Him, and which He had received from God, and which in them was the necessary result of their faith. Now, it is in the seeing of this life in those who proclaim the truth that the truth itself appears worthy of all acceptation, and that God verily, who has sent His Son to save sinners, is love. It is thus, you perceive, that the mission of the Church, whether of its ministers or its members, is not only to preach glad tidings, but to show their reality in their actual results; not only to preach salvation, but to preach it by saved men; not only to preach eternal life, but to preach it by those who possess it; not only to preach about a Father, but to reveal also that Father through His regenerated sons, who themselves know and love Him. Further, the idea of a Church is that of a society whose members are united through faith in the same truth, and are in possession of the same life. Such a society necessarily springs out of faith and love, and its members cannot choose but unite outwardly because united inwardly. Our Lord assumes its future existence and provides for its continuance. A Church realizing Christ's ideal would, therefore, possess, as its creed this, at least, of believing Christ's words, and the truth that "God had sent his Son to be the Savior of the world." For "every spirit that confesseth not that Christ hath come in the flesh is not of God." "And whosoever shall confess that Jesus is the Son of God, God dwelleth in him, and he in God." Its initiatory sacrament, that of baptism, does but express the nature of this society—viz., that its members are the children of God the Father through Christ the Son, and by the indwelling of the Holy Spirit—their character being a spiritual baptism into the possession of "God's name," which is "love."

Another characteristic of it is their possession of that eternal life which is exprest as well as maintained by the "communion" in which its members meet together as brethren, their bond of union being a common union with God in Christ and one another, through the constant partaking of Him, the living bread; eating His flesh and drinking His blood—that is, His whole life of self-sacrifice and love becoming a part of their very being. Worship in spirit and in truth is also necessarily involved in the idea of such a society; and I might add, worship, not from a command merely, but as a necessary result of spiritual character, becoming in a true sense "infallible" as to religion; but religion in this sense,—that of knowing God because of its members being able to say, "We know that he dwelleth in us, and we in him, because he hath given us his Spirit, and we know and testify that he sent his Son to be the Savior of the world." Such a Church would likewise, in a true sense, have an apostolical succession— that is, a succession of teachers and members who had the apostolic spirit, or the oneness as described by our Lord; for it would be able, from its possessing the Spirit of God, to discern those who were like-minded, and to select such as were specially fitted for the work of the ministry. This is the ideal of the Church.

But has such a Church been realized? Has there ever been a visible organized body of men who carried out this sublime purpose? Once, indeed, there was. For we perceive, more or less clearly, all these features in the early Church when it had received the Spirit on the day of Pentecost, and when its members met together and "had all things in common," and manifested such sonship towards God, and brotherhood towards each other; and sent forth everywhere its public minister and its members also to bring men into the same blessed unity. But supposing the ideal had no more been realized since that time than God's ideal as described by Moses had been fully realized in the Jewish Church;—yet must the ideal, nevertheless, be ever kept before the spiritual eye. For we do not produce high art by keeping a low rather than a high standard before the artist; neither can we reach to great things in the Church unless we keep a high standard before its members. It is unnecessary here to inquire how it came to pass that the Church, to such a great extent, lost this ideal as one visible society, and became so corrupt as to substitute innumerable vain appearances of spiritual realities for that which alone could satisfy a true and righteous God. But as things now are, the "Church" is broken up into various "churches" or societies, striving more or less to realize the ideal. Each society does so just in proportion as it is able to carry out our Lord's purpose as to its ministry being one in faith, believing Christ's words, in its knowing truly that He came from God to save sinners, and in its seeking, from love to God and man, to make all men know their Father, in the knowledge of whom is salvation.

But to confine myself to our own particular duties, let me remind you, fathers and brethren, of our high calling as profest ministers of Christ's Church. The cry of earnest souls, weary of their many burthens, unsatisfied with their husks, conscious of being in a distant land, and finding nothing which men can give to allay their hungering and thirsting, is this: "Show us the Father, and it sufficeth us!" Now supposing an earnest spirit, seeking after the Father, comes to us as His profest ministers in order to discover the truth of what we preach, he might very naturally say, "You preach to me a Savior who came a long time ago into the world professing to save sinners, and you tell me that He is coming again at some future period to judge the world and to bestow salvation upon many; but I want to know whether there is a Savior now; or is it all empty space between that past and that future? You tell me about salvation from the suffering of sin; I ask, 'Is there salvation from sin itself, without which I feel there can be no deliverance from suffering'? You tell me about a medicine that is an infallible cure for 'this ineradicable taint of sin,' and describe the terrible consequences of the disease to me if I be not cured, and the blessed results of joyous spiritual health and peace; but 'Can you show me any person who has actually been restored from disease to health by this divine medicine'? Is all this preaching a mere idle theory of life? Or if not, where is the life itself? Art thou thyself saved? If not—'physician, heal thyself'; for until then thou canst not cure me." But suppose, further, that this same person comes into close contact with the mind of the preacher, and that the more he sees and knows it the more he discerns in the man such thoughts regarding God, such a knowledge of Him, such a love to Him, as convince him that here at least is a reality and not a pretense; suppose that the more he discerns his whole inner life, the things which give him pain and joy, the things which he desires and loves, with his whole feelings towards his fellow-men—feelings expressed in a life of action, which, in spite of infirmities and shortcomings belonging to all human beings, the questioner cannot but recognize as a kind of life he never saw before—a life, too, which commends itself, from what it is, as being the most real and the most satisfactory to reason, conscience, and heart: can anything, I ask, be more calculated to convince him of the account which its possessor gives him as to its origin, when he says, "The life I now live in the flesh, I live by faith in the Son of God, who loved me, and gave himself for me." "It is a faithful saying, and worthy of all acceptation, that Christ came into the world to save sinners, of whom I am the chief." What then? What else must be the result of such a vision of true life than the conviction that God is our Father and that God is love, because it is evident from observation as well as from testimony that He hath sent His Son to save men, not in the past only, but to save them now—not to save only those who are called "good," but to save those who are the chief of sinners? If a man truly believes all this, then does he know God, and in so doing possesses eternal life. But more than this, how will his convictions be deepened if, in searching for others who may have the same life, and if, tho failing to discover any one visible body of Christians that show it forth in the unity of the Spirit and in the bond of peace, he is yet able to satisfy himself that there have been, during the last eighteen centuries, and that there are now, in every church, in every land, among all races of men, among those of different temperaments, different culture, and amidst a variety of all possible outward circumstances, men with like passions as himself, who have faith in the same Lord, and are thereby possest of a true love of God and of one another— how will this, I say, deepen in him the conviction that God is a Father, because a Savior, who "gave his Son, not that any should perish, but that all should possess everlasting life?" Will he not be thus led to "believe the record that God has given us eternal life, and that this life is in his Son?" I am persuaded that a man of the highest intellectual culture and the greatest learning, earnestly searching after God and Christ, and the truth of Christianity, would be more convinced of the love of the one as manifested in the truth of the other, by coming into contact with one true soul which, without perhaps intellectual culture or learning, yet truly loved God and man, than he would be by all the volumes on the evidence of Christianity ever written, without such a spiritual vision of a holy life.

On the other hand, supposing that no such evidence of the truth of Christianity could be discovered in the preacher of Christianity; nay, if his character contradicted his preaching; if, while he preached love to God and man, he manifested neither, but indifference, to say the least of it, to both; if, while he preached the necessity and the excellence of the Christian life, he himself revealed its very opposite—what effect would this have upon an earnest spirit, but that Christianity was a mere ideal system unsuited to the world, a philosophy of life that might be believed in, but not a life itself that might be possest?

This want of personal character, however imperfect, yet real, may account for the want of success in the mission of the Church to convince the world, whether at home or abroad. We may give religion but not godliness; the means of grace, as they are called, but not the grace seen and exprest in the living man. We would thus hear of Christianity without seeing it; hear about the love of God, and the love of Christ as a Savior, without being convinced even by those who send missionaries to India, who, altho they may individually reveal this life, yet how often are looked upon as mere official teachers; while the "Christians" from "Christendom" may, in coming into contact with the heathen, show by their denial of Christianity that it is a matter for the priesthood, not for all men; a book theology, but not an actual power working in humanity: and of such persons it may be said that they have profaned God's great name among the heathen.

And this, too, may also account for the secret of success by many a minister of whom the world knows nothing: "For greatest minds are those of whom the noisy world hears least." They may not be great in the ordinary sense of the word—great as thinkers, great as orators, or great in the possession of any remarkable gifts; but they are nevertheless great in the kingdom of heaven; great because little children—great in meekness, in patience, in humility, in love of God and man, and who carry this music in their heart, "through dusky land and wrangling mart." What is the secret of their power? What but an eternal reality! the reality of a godly, godlike life obtained from God, and sustained by God, and seen in the eye, felt in the hand, heard in the words—a light of life which shines beside many a dying bed in many a home of sorrow, as well as in the pulpit. This is a kind of life whose biography will be written with the tears of the grateful orphan and widow, and of many a saved soul which remembers its possessor as its spiritual father. Such a ministry as this can no more fail than the love of God which gives it birth. Let us thank God, therefore, that such a secret power as this is within the reach of us all. We may not be men of talent, and for that we are not responsible; but we may be good men because little children towards God, and for that we are responsible: "I thank thee, heavenly Father, that thou hast hid these things from the wise and prudent, and revealed them unto babes."

And now, fathers and brethren, such is our high calling, to proclaim the glad tidings that God has sent Christ into the world to save sinners. Our chief authority for doing this is that we know it to be true; and if so, no one can deprive us of the high privilege and joy of proclaiming it. A glorious work is thus given us to do; we are ambassadors for God, beseeching men to be reconciled to Him, and we are fellow-workers with our Lord Himself. But this involves a great responsibility, corresponding to the greatness of our calling. For it is at once a glorious and a tremendous thought that Christ perils the chief evidence of the truth of Christianity, not upon what we say, but more upon what we are; and what we are is neither more nor less than what God knows us to be. Our preaching may, nevertheless, fail in some cases to convince the world, as it has done before; for the glory of Christ Himself was not seen by Judas. Indeed the light of life, when it shines, requires the single eye to see it. But in so far as the ministry of men, as an instrumentality, can convince the world, let our ministry be such as is calculated according to Christ's purpose to produce this result. Let it consist of those who can say, "We know whom we have believed." "We know and believe the love that God hath to us." "We testify that he sent his Son to be the Savior of the world."

But I must bring my sermon to a close.

Pardon me, my brethren, if I have appeared to address you in any other spirit than that of one who would with you confess his sins and shortcomings, and lament with shame and sorrow how much time and power have been lost never to be regained; how many gifts and noble opportunities have been neglected and perverted through unbelief and sloth, which might have been used for our own good and that of our fellow-men. Verily the day is far spent with many of us, and the night is near in which no man can work. Whatever our hands find to do must be done now or never. Let us pray that the living Spirit of God, given to all who seek Him, and whose work it is to glorify the Son, may take of His things and show them to our souls, and open our spiritual eye to see the glory of God in the face of Christ, so that we may be changed into the same glory. May we strive to keep the unity of the Spirit in the bond of peace, and be enabled so to preach and so to live that the world may be convinced, by what it sees and hears, of the reality of the love of God the Father in giving us and all men eternal life through Jesus Christ His Son! May He who makes us sons of God enable us, as sons, to be glorified in the perfection and revelation of our characters, so that with our elder Brother we may glorify His Father and our Father!

And now, to Father, Son and Holy Ghost, one God, be glory, dominion, and praise for evermore. Amen!

MOZLEY

THE REVERSAL OF HUMAN JUDGMENT

BIOGRAPHICAL NOTE

James B. Mozley, English divine and philosopher, was born at Gainsborough, Lincolnshire, in 1813. He was educated at Oxford, and is particularly known for his discourses on Baptism and Predestination. Gladstone appointed him as professor of divinity at Oxford. His Bampton Lectures on Miracles (1863) are still considered of classical authority. Dr. Brastow, in speaking of his clear and well-ordered thought, says: "He was intent upon getting at the heart of all subjects investigated, and his slowness in clearing up a subject and his deliberation and fastidiousness with respect to his diction embarrassed him. The result was a mastery of thought and an exactness and clearness and strength of speech that are more than an offset for the difficulties he encountered; and one can hardly fail to see that this patient, self-poised mental habit saved him from one-sidedness and kept the balance of his judgement and made him the safer guide. We see here the immense value of thorough mental training." He died in 1878.

MOZLEY

1813-1878
THE REVERSAL OF HUMAN JUDGMENT[3]

Many that are first shall be last; and the last shall be first.
—Matthew xix., 30.

Perhaps there is hardly any person of reflection to whom the thought has not occurred at times, of the final judgment turning out to be a great subversion of human estimates of men. Society forms its opinions of men, and places some on a high pinnacle; they are favorites with it, religious and moral favorites. Such judgments are a necessary and proper part of the present state of things; they are so, quite independently of the question whether they are true or not; it is proper that there should be this sort of expression of the voice of the day; the world is not nothing, because it is transient; it must judge and speak upon such evidence as it has, and is capable of seeing. Therefore those characters of men are by all means to be respected by us, as members of this world; they have their place, they are a part of the system. But does the idea strike us of some enormous subversion of human judgments in the next world, some vast rectification, to realize which now, even if we could, would not be good for us? Such an idea would not be without support from some of those characteristic prophetic sayings of our Lord, which, like the slanting strokes of the sun's rays across the clouds, throw forward a tract of mysterious light athwart the darkness of the future. Such is that saying in which a shadow of the Eternal

---

3   By permission of the publishers, Messrs. Longmans, Green & Co.

Judgment seems to come over us—"Many that are first shall be last; and the last shall be first." It is impossible to read this saying without an understanding that it was intended to throw an element of wholesome scepticism into the present estimate of human character, and to check the idolatry of the human heart which lifts up its favorites with as much of self-complacency as of enthusiasm, and in its worship of others flatters itself.

Indeed, this language of Scripture, which speaks of the subversion of human judgments in another world, comes in connection with another language with which it most remarkably fits in, language which speaks very decidedly of a great deception of human judgments in this world. It is observable that the gospel prophecy of the earthly future of Christianity is hardly what we should have expected it beforehand to be; there is a great absence of brightness in it; the sky is overcast with clouds, and birds of evil omen fly to and fro; there is an agitation of the air, as if dark elements were at work in it; or it is as if a fog rose up before our eyes, and treacherous lights were moving to and fro in it, which we could not trust. Prophecy would fain presage auspiciously, but as soon as she casts her eye forward, her note saddens, and the chords issue in melancholy and sinister cadences which depress the hearer's mind. And what is the burden of her strain? It is this. As soon as ever Christianity is cast into the world to begin its history, that moment there begins a great deception. It is a pervading thought in gospel prophecy—the extraordinary capacity for deceiving and being deceived that would arise under the gospel; it is spoken of as something peculiar in the world. There are to be false Christs and false prophets, false signs and wonders; many that will come in Christ's name, saying, I am Christ, and deceive many; so that it is the parting admonition of Christ to His disciples—"Take heed, lest any man deceive you"— as if that would be the greater danger. And this great quantity of deception was to culminate in that one in whom all power of signs and lying wonders should reside, even that Antichrist, who as God should sit in the temple of God, showing himself that he is God. Thus before the true Christ was known to the world, the prophecy of the false one was implanted deep in the heart of Christianity.

When we come to the explanation of this mass of deception as it applies to the Christian society, and the conduct of Christians, we find that it consists of a great growth of specious and showy effects, which will in fact issue out of Christianity, not implying sterling goodness. Christianity will act as a great excitement to human nature, it will communicate a great impulse, it will move and stir man's feelings and intellect; this impulse will issue in a great variety of high gifts and activities, much zeal and ardor. But this brilliant manifestation will be to a large extent lacking in the substance of the Christian character. It will be a great show. That is to say, there will be underneath it the deceitful human heart— the *natura callida*, as Thomas á Kempis calls it, *quæ se semper pro fine habet*. We have even in the early Christian Church that specious display of gifts which put aside as secondary the more solid part of religion, and which St. Paul had so strongly to check. Gospel prophecy goes remarkably in this direction, as to what Christianity would do in the world; that it would not only bring out the truth of human nature, but would, like some powerful alchemy, elicit and extract the falsehood of it; that it would not only develop what was sincere and sterling in man, but what was counterfeit in him too. Not that Christianity favors falsehood, any more than the law favored sin because it brought out sin. The law, as St. Paul says, brought out sin because it was spiritual, and forced sin to be sin against light. So in the case of Christianity. If a very high, pure, and heart-searching religion is brought into contact with a corrupt nature, the nature grasps at the greatness of the religion, but will not give up itself; yet to unite the two requires a self-deception the more subtle and potent in proportion to the purity of the religion. And certainly, comparing the hypocrisy of the Christian with that of the old world, we see that the one was a weak production in comparison with the other, which is indeed a very powerful creation; throwing itself into feeling and language with an astonishing freedom and elasticity, and possessing wonderful spring and largeness.

There is, however, one very remarkable utterance of our Lord Himself upon this subject, which deserves special attention. "Many will say to me in that day, Lord, Lord, have we not prophesied in thy name, and in thy name cast out devils, and in thy name done many wonderful works? And then I will profess unto them, I never knew you." Now this is a very remarkable prophecy, for one reason, that in the very first start of Christianity, upon the very threshold of its entrance into the world, it looks through its success and universal reception, into an ulterior result of that victory—a counterfeit profession of it. It sees, before the first nakedness of its birth is over, a prosperous and flourishing religion,which it is worth while for others to pay homage to, because it reflects credit on its champions. Our Lord anticipates the time when active zeal for Himself will be no guaranty. And we may observe the difference between Christ and human founders. The latter are too glad of any zeal in their favor, to examine very strictly the tone and quality of it. They grasp at it at once; not so our Lord. He does not want it even for Himself, unless it is pure in the individual. But this statement of our Lord's is principally important, as being a prophecy relating to the earthly future of Christianity. It places before us public religious leaders, men of influence in the religious world, who spread and push forward by gifts of eloquence and powers of mind, the truths of His religion, whom yet He will not accept, because of a secret corruptness in the aim and spirit with which they did their work. The prophecy puts forth before us the fact of a great deal of work being done in the Church, and outwardly good zealous work, upon the same motive in substance, upon which worldly men do their work in the world, and stamps it as the activity of corrupt nature. The rejection of this class of religious workers is complete, altho they have been, as the language itself declares, forward and active for spiritual objects, and not only had them on their lips.

Here then we have a remarkable subversion of human judgments in the next world foretold by our Lord Himself; for those men certainly come forward with established religious characters to which they appeal; they have no doubt of their position in God's kingdom, and they speak with the air of men whose claims have been acquiesced in by others, and by numbers. And thus a false Christian growth is looked to in gospel prophecy, which will be able to meet even the religious tests of the current day, and sustain its pretensions, but which will not satisfy the tests of the last day.

We are then perhaps at first surprized at the sternness of their sentence, and are ready to say with the trembling disciple, "Who then shall be saved?" But when we reflect upon it, we shall see that it is not more than what meets the case; i. e., that we know of sources of error in the estimate of human character which will account for great mistakes being made; which mistakes will have to be rectified.

One source of mistakes then is, that while the gospel keeps to one point of its classification of men,—viz., the motive, by which alone it decides their character, the mass of men in fact find it difficult to do so. They have not that firm hold of the moral idea which prevents them from wandering from it, and being diverted by irrelevant considerations, they think of the spirituality of a man as belonging to the department to which he is attached, the profession he makes, the subject matter he works upon, the habitual language he has to use. The sphere of these men, of whom the estimate was to be finally reversed, was a religious one,—viz., the Church, and this was a remarkable prop to them. Now, with respect to this, it must be observed that the Church is undoubtedly in its design a spiritual society, but it is also a society of this world as well; and it depends upon the inward motive of a man whether it is to him a spiritual society or a worldly one. The Church, as soon as ever it is embodied in a visible collection or society of men, who bring into it human nature, with human influences, regards, points of view, estimates, aims, and objects—I say the Church, from the moment it thus embodies itself in a human society, is the world. Individual souls in it convert into reality the high profest principles of the body, but the active stock of motives in it are the motives of human nature. Can the visible Church indeed afford to do without these motives? Of course it cannot. It must do its work by means of these to a great extent, just as the world does its work. Religion itself is beautiful and heavenly, but the machinery for it is very like the machinery for anything else. I speak of the apparatus for conducting and administering the visible system of it. Is not the machinery for all causes and objects much the same, communication with others, management, contrivance, combination, adaptation of means to end? Religion then is itself a painful struggle, but religious machinery provides as pleasant a form of activity as any other machinery possesses; and it counts for and exercises much the same kind of talents and gifts that the machinery of any other department does, that of a government office, or a public institution, or a large business. The Church, as a part of the work, must have active-minded persons to conduct its policy and affairs; which persons must, by their very situation, connect themselves with spiritual subjects, as being the subjects of the society; they must express spiritual joys, hopes, and fears, apprehensions, troubles, trials, aims, and wishes. These are topics which belong to the Church as a department. A religious society, then, or religious sphere of action, or religious sphere of subjects, is irrelevant as regards the spirituality of the individual person, which is a matter of inward motive.

One would not of course exclude from the sphere of religion the motive of *esprit de corps*: it is undoubtedly a great stimulus, and in its measure is consistent with all simplicity and singleness of heart; but in an intense form, when the individual is absorbed in a blind obedience to a body, it corrupts the quality of religion; it ensnares the man in a kind of self-interest; and he sees in the success of the body the reflection of himself. It becomes an egotistic motive. There has been certainly an immense produce from it; but the type of religion it has produced is a deflection from simplicity; it may possess striking and powerful qualities, but it is not like the free religion of the heart; and there is that difference between the two, which there is between what comes from a second-hand source and from the fountain head. It has not that naturalness (in the highest sense) which alone gives beauty to religion.

Again, those who feel that they have a mission may convert it into a snare to themselves. Doubtless, if, according to St. Paul, "he who desireth the office of a bishop desireth a good work," so one who has a mission to do some particular work has a good office given him. Still, where life is too prominently regarded in this light, the view of life as a mission tends to supersede the view of it as trial and probation. The mission becomes the final cause of life. The generality may be born to do their duty in that station of life in which it has pleased God to call them; but in their own case the mission overtops and puts into the shade the general purpose of life as probation; the generality are sent into the world for their own moral benefit, but they are rather sent into the world for the benefit of that world itself. The outward object with its display and machinery is apt to reduce to a kind of insignificance the inward individual end of life. It appears small and commonplace. The success of their own individual probation is assumed in embarking upon the larger work, as the less is included in the greater; it figures as a preliminary in their eyes, which may be taken for granted; it appears an easy thing to them to save their own souls, a thing, so to speak, for anybody to do.

What has been dwelt upon hitherto as a source of false magnifying and exaltation of human character, has been the invisibility of men's motives. But let us take another source of mistake in human judgment.

Nothing is easier, when we take gifts of the intellect and imagination in the abstract, than to see that these do not constitute moral goodness. This is indeed a mere truism; and yet, in the concrete, it is impossible not to see how nearly they border upon counting as such; to what advantage they set off any moral good there may be in a man; sometimes even supplying the absence of real good with what looks extremely like it. On paper these mental gifts are a mere string of terms; we see exactly what these terms denote, and we cannot mistake it for something else. It is plain that eloquence, imagination, poetical talent, are no more moral goodness than riches are, or than health and strength are, or than noble birth is. We know that bad men have possest them just as much as good men. Nevertheless, take them in actual life, in the actual effect and impression they make, as they express a man's best moods and highest perceptions and feelings, and what a wonderful likeness and image of what is moral do they produce. Think of the effect of refined power of expression, of a keen and vivid imagination as applied to the illustration and enrichment of moral subjects,—to bringing out, e. g., with the whole force of intellectual sympathy, the delicate and high regions of character,—does not one who can do this seem to have all the goodness which he expresses? And it is quite possible he may have; but this does not prove it. There is nothing more in this than the faculty of imagination and intelligent appreciation of moral things. There enters thus unavoidably often into a great religious reputation a good deal which is not religion, but power.

Let us take the character which St. Paul draws. It is difficult to believe that one who had the tongue of men and of angels would not be able to persuade the world that he himself was extraordinarily good. Rather it is part of the fascination of the gift, that the grace of it is reflected in the possessor. But St. Paul gives him, besides thrilling speech which masters men's spirits and carries them away, those profound depths of imagination which still and solemnize them; which lead them to the edge of the unseen world, and excite the sense of the awful and supernatural; he has the understanding of all mysteries. And again, knowledge unfolds all its stores to him with which to illustrate and enrich spiritual truths. Let one then, so wonderful in mental gifts, combine them with the utmost fervor, with boundless faith, before which everything gives way; boundless zeal, ready to make even splendid sacrifices; has there been any age in which such a man would have been set down as sounding and empty? St. Paul could see that such a man might yet be without the true substance—goodness; and that all his gifts could not guarantee it to him; but to the mass his own eloquence would interpret him, the gifts would carry the day, and the brilliant partial virtues would disguise the absence of the general grace of love.

Gifts of intellect and imagination, poetical power, and the like, are indeed in themselves a department of worldly prosperity. It is a very narrow view of prosperity that it consists only in having property; a certain kind of gifts are just as much worldly prosperity as riches; nor are they less so if they belong to a religious man, any more than riches are less prosperity because a religious man is rich. We call these gifts worldly prosperity, because they are in themselves a great advantage, and create success, influence, credit, and all which man so much values; and at the same time they are not moral goodness, because the most corrupt men may have them.

But even the gifts of outward fortune themselves have much of the effect of gifts of mind in having the semblance of something moral. They set off what goodness a man has to such immense advantage, and heighten the effect of it. Take some well-disposed person, and suppose him suddenly to be left an enormous fortune, he would feel himself immediately so much better a man. He would seem to himself to become suddenly endowed with a new large-heartedness and benevolence. He would picture himself the generous patron, the large dispenser of charity, the promoter of all good in the world. The power to become such would look like a new disposition. And in the eyes of the others, too, his goodness would appear to have taken a fresh start. Even serious piety is recognized more as such; it is brought out and placed in high relief, when connected with outward advantages; and so the gifts of fortune become a kind of moral addition to a man.

Action, then, on a large scale, and the overpowering effect of great gifts, are what produce, in a great degree, what we call the canonization of men—the popular judgment which sets them up morally and spiritually upon the pinnacle of the temple, and which professes to be a forestalment, through the mouth of the Church or of religious society, of the final judgment. How decisive is the world's, and, not less confident, the visible Church's note of praise. It is just that trumpet note which does not bear a doubt. How it is trusted! With what certainty it speaks! How large a part of the world's and Church's voice is praise! It is an immense and ceaseless volume of utterance. And by all means let man praise man, and not do it grudgingly either; let there be an echo of that vast action which goes on in the world, provided we only speak of what we know. But if we begin to speak of what we do not know, and which only a higher judgment can decide, we are going beyond our province. On this question we are like men who are deciding irreversibly on some matter in which everything depends upon one element in the case, which element they cannot get at. We appear to know a great deal of one another, and yet, if we reflect, what a vast system of secrecy the moral world is. How low down in a man sometimes (not always) lies the fundamental motive which sways his life? But this is what everything depends on. Is it an unspiritual motive? Is there some keen passion connected with this world at the bottom? Then it corrupts the whole body of action. There is a good deal of prominent religion then, which keeps up its character, even when this motive betrays itself; great gifts fortify it, and people do not see because they will not. But at any rate there is a vast quantity of religious position which has this one great point undecided beneath it; and we know of tremendous dangers to which it is exposed. Action upon a theater may doubtless be as simple-minded action as any other; it has often been; it has been often even childlike action; the apostles acted on a theater; they were a spectacle to men and to angels. Still, what dangers in a spiritual point of view does it ordinarily include—dangers to simplicity, inward probity, sincerity! How does action on this scale and of this kind seem, notwithstanding its religious object, to pass over people, not touching one of their faults, leaving—more than their infirmities—the dark veins of evil in their character as fixed as ever. How will persons sacrifice themselves to their objects? They would benefit the world, it would appear, at their own moral expense; but this is a kind of generosity which is perilous policy for the soul, and is indeed the very mint in which the great mass of false spiritual coinage is made.

On the other hand, while the open theater of spiritual power and energy is so accessible to corrupt motives, which, tho undermining its truthfulness, leave standing all the brilliance of the outer manifestation; let it be considered what a strength and power of goodness may be accumulating in unseen quarters. The way in which man bears temptation is what decides his character; yet how secret is the system of temptation? Who knows what is going on? What the real ordeal has been? What its issue was? So with respect to the trial of griefs and sorrows, the world is again a system of secrecy. There is something particularly penetrating, and which strikes home, in those disappointments which are especially not extraordinary, and make no show. What comes naturally and as a part of our situation has a probing force grander strokes have not; there is a solemnity and stateliness in these, but the blow which is nearest to common life gets the stronger hold. Is there any particular event which seems to have, if we may say so, a kind of malice in it which provokes the Manichean feeling in our nature, it is something which we should have a difficulty in making appear to any one else any special trial. Compared with this inner grasp of some stroke of providence, voluntary sacrifice stands outside of us. After all, the self-made trial is a poor disciplinarian weapon; there is a subtle masterly irritant and provoking point in the genuine natural trial, and in the natural crossness of events, which the artificial thing cannot manage; we can no more make our trials than we can make our feelings. In this way moderate deprivations are in some cases more difficult to bear than extreme ones. "I can bear total obscurity," says Pascal, "well enough; what disgusts me is semi-obscurity; I can make an idol of the whole, but no great merit of the half." And so it is often the case that what we must do as simply right, and which would not strike even ourselves, and still less anybody else, is just the hardest thing to do. A work of supererogation would be much easier. All this points in the direction of great work going on under common outsides where it is not noticed; it hints at a secret sphere of growth and progress; and as such it is an augury and presage of a harvest which may come some day suddenly to light, which human judgments had not counted on.

It is upon such a train of thought as this which has been passing through our minds that we raise ourselves to the reception of that solemn sentence which Scripture has inscribed on the curtain which hangs down before the judgment-seat—"The first shall be last, and the last shall be first." The secrets of the tribunal are guarded, and yet a finger points which seems to say—"Beyond, in this direction, behind this veil, things are different from what you will have looked for."

Suppose, e. g., any supernatural judge should appear in the world now, and it is evident that the scene he would create would be one to startle us; we should not soon be used to it; it would look strange; it would shock and appal; and that from no other cause than simply its reductions; that it presented characters stripped bare, denuded of what was irrelevant to goodness, and only with their moral substance left. The judge would take no cognizance of a rich imagination, power of language, poetical gifts and the like, in themselves, as parts of goodness, any more than he would of riches and prosperity; and the moral residuum would appear perhaps a bare result. The first look of divine justice would strike us as injustice; it would be too pure a justice for us; we should be long in reconciling ourselves to it. Justice would appear, like the painter's gaunt skeleton of emblematic meaning, to be stalking through the world, smiting with attenuation luxuriating forms of virtue. Forms, changed from what we knew, would meet us, strange unaccustomed forms, and we should have to ask them who they are—"You were flourishing but a short while ago, what has happened to you now?" And the answer, if it spoke the truth, would be—"Nothing, except that now, much which lately counted as goodness, counts as such no longer; we are tried by a new moral measure, out of which we issue different men; gifts which have figured as goodness remain as gifts, but cease to be goodness." Thus would the large sweep made of human canonizations act like blight or volcanic fire upon some rich landscape, converting the luxury of nature into a dried-up scene of bare stems and scorched vegetation.

So may the scrutiny of the last day, by discovering the irrelevant material in men's goodness, reduce to a shadow much exalted earthly character. Men are made up of professions, gifts, and talents, and also of themselves, but all so mixed together that we cannot separate one element from another; but another day must show what the moral substance is, and what is only the brightness and setting off of gifts. On the other hand, the same day may show where, tho the setting off of gifts is less, the substance is more. If there will be reversal of human judgment for evil, there will be reversal of it for good too. The solid work which has gone on in secret, under common exteriors, will then spring into light, and come out in a glorious aspect. Do we not meet with surprizes of this kind here, which look like auguries of a greater surprize in the next world, a surprize on a vast scale. Those who have lived under an exterior of rule, when they come to a trying moment sometimes disappoint us; they are not equal to the act required from them; because their forms of duty, whatever they are, have not touched in reality their deeper fault of character, meanness, or jealousy, or the like, but have left them where they were; they have gone on thinking themselves good because they did particular things, and used certain language, and adopted certain ways of thought, and have been utterly unconscious all the time of a corroding sin within them. On the other hand, some one who did not promise much, comes out at a moment of trial strikingly and favorably. This is a surprize, then, which sometimes happens, nay, and sometimes a greater surprize still, when out of the eater comes forth meat, and out of a state of sin there springs the soul of virtue. The act of the thief on the cross is a surprize. Up to the time when he was judged he was a thief, and from a thief he became a saint. For even in the dark labyrinth of evil there are unexpected outlets; sin is established by the habit in the man, but the good principle which is in him also, but kept down and supprest, may be secretly growing too; it may be undermining it, and extracting the life and force from it. In this man, then, sin becomes more and more, tho holding its place by custom, an outside and a coating, just as virtue does in the deteriorating man, till at last, by a sudden effort and the inspiration of an opportunity, the strong good casts off the weak crust of evil and comes out free. We witness a conversion.

But this is a large and mysterious subject—the foundation for high virtue to become apparent in a future world, which hardly rises up above the ground here. We cannot think of the enormous trial which is undergone in this world by vast masses without the thought also of some sublime fruit to come of it some day. True, it may not emerge from the struggle of bare endurance here, but has not the seed been sown? Think of the burden of toil and sorrow borne by the crowds of poor: we know that pain does not of itself make people good; but what we observe is, that even in those in whom the trial seems to do something, it yet seems such a failure. What inconstancy, violence, untruths! The pathos in it all moves you. What a tempest of character it is! And yet when such trial has been passed we involuntarily say—has not a foundation been laid? And so in the life of a soldier, what agonies must nature pass through in it! While the present result of such a trial is so disappointing, so little seems to come of it! Yet we cannot think of what has been gone through by countless multitudes in war, of the dreadful altar of sacrifice, and the lingering victims, without the involuntary idea arising that in some, even of the irregular and undisciplined, the foundation of some great purification has been laid. We hear sometimes of single remarkable acts of virtue, which spring from minds in which there is not the habit of virtue. Such acts point to a foundation, a root of virtue in man, deeper than habit; they are sudden leaps which show an unseen spring, which are able to compress in a moment the growth of years.

To conclude. The gospel language throws doubt upon the final stability of much that passes current here with respect to character, upon established judgments, and the elevations of the outward sanctuary. It lays down a wholesome scepticism. We do not do justice to the spirit of the gospel by making it enthusiastic simply, or even benevolent simply. It is sagacious, too. It is a book of judgment. Man is judged in it. Our Lord is Judge. We cannot separate our Lord's divinity from His humanity; and yet we must be blind if we do not see a great judicial side of our Lord's human character;—that severe type of understanding, in relation to the worldly man, which has had its imperfect representation in great human minds. He was unspeakably benevolent, kind, compassionate; true, but He was a Judge. It was indeed of His very completeness as man that He should know man; and to know is to judge. He must be blind who, in the significant acts and sayings of our Lord as they unroll themselves in the pregnant page of the gospel, does not thus read His character; he sees it in that insight into pretensions, exposure of motives, laying bare of disguises; in the sayings—"Believe it not"; "Take heed that no man deceive you"; "Behold, I have told you"; in all that profoundness of reflection in regard to man, which great observing minds among mankind have shown, tho accompanied by much of frailty, anger, impatience, or melancholy. His human character is not benevolence only; there is in it wise distrust— that moral sagacity which belongs to the perfection of man.

Now then, as has been said, this scepticism with regard to human character has had, as a line of thought, certain well-known representatives in great minds, who have discovered a root of selfishness in men's actions, have probed motives, extracted aims, and placed man before himself denuded and exposed; they judged him, and in the frigid sententiousness or the wild force of their utterances, we hear that of which we cannot but say, how true! But knowledge is a goad to those who have it; a disturbing power; a keenness which distorts; and in the sight it gives it partly blinds also. The fault of these minds was that in exposing evil they did not really believe in goodness; goodness was to them but an airy ideal, the dispirited echo of perplexed hearts,—returned to them from the rocks of the desert, without bearing hope with it. They had no genuine belief in any world which was different from theirs; they availed themselves of an ideal indeed to judge this world, and they could not have judged it without; for anything, whatever it is, is good, if we have no idea of anything better; and therefore the conception of a good world was necessary to judge the bad one. But the ideal held loose to their minds—not anything to be substantiated, not as a type in which a real world was to be cast, not as anything of structural power, able to gather into it, form round it, and build up upon itself; not, in short, as anything of power at all, able to make anything, or do anything, but only like some fragrant scent in the air, which comes and goes, loses itself, returns again in faint breaths, and rises and falls in imperceptive waves. Such was goodness to these minds; it was a dream. But the gospel distrust is not disbelief in goodness. It raises a great suspense, indeed, it shows a curtain not yet drawn up, it checks weak enthusiasm, it appends a warning note to the pomp and flattery of human judgments, to the erection of idols; and points to a day of great reversal; a day of the Lord of Hosts; the day of pulling down and plucking up, of planting and building. But, together with the law of sin, the root of evil in the world, and the false goodness in it, it announces a fount of true natures; it tells us of a breath of Heaven of which we know not whence it cometh and whither it goeth; which inspires single individual hearts, that spring up here and there, and everywhere, like broken gleams of the supreme goodness. And it recognizes in the renewed heart of man an instinct which can discern true goodness and distinguish it from false; a secret discrimination in the good by which they know the good. It does not therefore stand in the way of that natural and quiet reliance which we are designed by God to have in one another, and that trust in those whose hearts we know. "Wisdom is justified of her children"; "My sheep hear my voice, but a stranger will they not follow, for they know not the voice of strangers."

END OF VOLUME V

www.ingramcontent.com/pod-product-compliance
Lightning Source LLC
Chambersburg PA
CBHW031958010726
47493CB00007B/2249